# DISCARD

# The Wild Duck Chase

*Oops: 20 Life Lessons from the Fiascoes That Shaped America,*
with coauthor Patrick J. Kiger
*Poplorica: A Popular History of the Fads, Mavericks, Inventions,*
*and Lore That Shaped Modern America,*
with coauthor Patrick J. Kiger
*Straw Men* (2002 Edgar Award nominee)
*Shadow Image*
*Time Release* (1998 Anthony Award nominee)

# The Wild Duck Chase

*Inside the Strange and Wonderful World of
the Federal Duck Stamp Contest*

## Martin J. Smith

Walker & Company
New York

Published by Walker Publishing Company, Inc., New York
A Division of Bloomsbury Publishing

3/13   H  25

All papers used by Walker & Company are natural, recyclable products made
from wood grown in well-managed forests. The manufacturing processes
conform to the environmental regulations of the country of origin.

LIBRARY OF CONGRESS CATALOGING-IN-PUBLICATION DATA
HAS BEEN APPLIED FOR.

ISBN: 978-0-8027-7952-6

Visit Walker & Company's website at www.walkerbooks.com

First U.S. edition 2012

1 3 5 7 9 10 8 6 4 2

Typeset by Westchester Book Group
Printed in the U.S.A. by Quad/Graphics, Fairfield, Pennsylvania

To Judy

The beautiful creature, like the mountain, is there—the bird to be painted, the mountain climbed. The bird's beauty must be acknowledged, understood, captured. *I am the one to capture it*, says the bird-artist: *I shall do the best I can.*

—ORNITHOLOGIST AND LEGENDARY WILDLIFE ARTIST GEORGE MIKSCH SUTTON, FROM HIS 1962 ESSAY "IS BIRD-ART ART?"

I gotta get it out of there. She really doesn't like it.

—TWO-TIME FEDERAL DUCK STAMP ARTIST ROBERT HAUTMAN, ON HIS WIFE'S MISGIVINGS ABOUT THE SPREAD-EAGLED PHEASANT IN HIS SEARS KENMORE FREEZER, ALONG WITH FOURTEEN OTHER DEAD BIRDS, APRIL 24, 2010

# CONTENTS

# PROLOGUE

NOTHING AT THE corner of North Fairfax Drive and Vermont Street in Arlington, Virginia, suggests that the nondescript building at 4401 North Fairfax houses anything extraordinary, much less the three-office suite of one of the best ideas America's federal government has ever had. Even after a four-floor elevator ride, it's tricky to find the headquarters of the Federal Duck Stamp Program in the small labyrinth occupied by the Division of Bird Habitat Conservation, which itself is a thirty-employee subnode of the U.S. Fish and Wildlife Service, which is part of the Department of the Interior.

Duck Stamp Program chief Patricia Fisher's guided tour takes all of two minutes.

If you pause during that tour, though, you'll notice clues to a story that, told in full, might restore your faith in the often ineffective and inefficient U.S. government. The walls are hung with framed prints of painted ducks, including past winners of the Federal Duck Stamp Contest, the centerpiece of the program's peculiar magic. You also might notice a placard between the offices of Duck Stamp stalwarts Elizabeth Jackson and Laurie Shaffer that reads, "Well-behaved women rarely make history," and, on Shaffer's office wall, a framed stencil of a floating duck accompanied by the words "Behave like a duck. Stay calm on the surface but paddle like crazy underneath."

Those three women run the $852,000-a-year program, which in 2010 generated about $24 million in revenue[1] through the sale of an obscure revenue stamp to a dwindling number of hunters and stamp collectors, and to what they hope is a growing number of enlightened birders and other conservationists. Since it began in 1934, what Fisher calls "the little program that could" has generated more than $750 million, and ninety-eight cents of each dollar has been used to help purchase or lease 5.3 million acres of waterfowl habitat in the United States, with much of that land now protected within the National Wildlife Refuge System.[2]

And yet, by the summer of 2010, Fisher was worried, and not just because the recent Deepwater Horizon rig explosion and subsequent, ongoing BP oil spill in the Gulf of Mexico were temporarily consuming the attention and resources of the Fish and Wildlife Service, of which her program is a very small part. Her concern was a more chronic condition.

Since assuming leadership of the program in 2005, Fisher had been scrambling to educate the largely unaware American public about the value of the Federal Duck Stamp Program, and to remind Congress, which controls its funding, not only that the program is effective but also that it even exists. The program operates so efficiently and so far off the federal bureaucratic radar that a Freedom of Information Act request for any audits, white papers, or similar assessment reports on the program's efficacy triggers a kind of confounded head-scratching among Washington officialdom.

In April 2010, Fisher went to St. Paul, Minnesota, to oversee the final judging of the Junior Duck Stamp Contest, a smaller-scale federal art competition designed to introduce the program to a nation of children these days primarily focused on iPods and Facebook rather than wild waterfowl and acrylic paints. She has the look and demeanor of a stern high school teacher, which, with her master's degree in history, she could have been. Maybe it was her natural reverence for the past, or maybe she was just exhausted after the conclusion of the contest judging that evening, but she clearly was grappling with questions about the program's future.

"The Duck Stamp Program is a relic from a different era," she said. "How to make it modern? That's the challenge. That's what keeps me up at night: doing the best we can to treasure our program and making sure other people appreciate it for what it is, how special it is."

The program was started by environmental visionaries in the middle of the Dust Bowl era and the Great Depression, when the need to conserve resources for waterfowl seemed a frivolous pursuit in a nation desperate to simply feed itself. With real and raw emotion in her voice, Fisher added, "I just really respect those people at the creation [of the program] and honor their memories. What they did was amazing to me. Everything worked. It was a tragic time for people, and wildlife. But some amazing things came out of that. Not only the Duck Stamp Program but the federal Work Projects Administration, the Civilian Conservation Corps, things like that. We have really historic roots, and it all came out of this tragic time."

Fisher paused, then peered over the top edge of her rimless eyeglasses. "I don't want all that to go. It would be a terrible thing to lose."

# 1

# THE HUNTERS GATHER

AT NINE A.M. on October 15, 2010, when the doors of the David Brower Center—the self-proclaimed "greenest building in Berkeley [California]"—officially open to the public for the day's event, there's no hint of trouble. Four months earlier, the *San Francisco Chronicle* previewed the upcoming 2010 Federal Duck Stamp Contest on its website with a story whose headline predicted, somewhat darkly, that Berkeley, the American epicenter of dissent and protest, was "the place most likely to get its plumage in a bunch" over a gathering primarily made up of people who consider shooting waterfowl to be a sport. The *Chronicle* piece made clear that the event—a dramatic two-day process involving three scheduled elimination rounds—was likely to offend local sensibilities.[1]

To be sure, all the necessary ingredients for a culture clash are in place. Just two years earlier, an epic struggle for conservation played out in Berkeley, where any perceived assault on nature is a reason to break out the protest signs. The contest site is located a few hundred yards away from that of the longest urban tree-sit in American history, which pitted a small band of conservationists against the University of California, Berkeley.

The tree huggers—the term isn't used pejoratively here, but literally—moved into the treetops and stayed there for more than twenty months, between December 2, 2006, and September 9, 2008. They were determined to prevent the school from cutting down a beloved grove of oak trees to build an athletic training facility.[2]

Now, inside the Brower Center—a temple to environmental activism named after one of the twentieth century's greatest conservation pioneers and located directly across Oxford Street from the UC Berkeley campus—the 180-seat auditorium is beginning to fill. To the local tree-sitters and the eco-warriors who supported them, it must seem like the barbarians are at the gates.

Members of Audubon California are mingling with hunters—two groups that some people consider sworn enemies. Most of the artists in the room are avid hunters as well. One, a previous contest winner, is just back from a three-week trip to Montana, where he bow-hunted for elk, and is planning a duck-hunting trip to Manitoba, Canada. Another previous winner, roaring with laughter, months earlier had regaled two fellow hunters with a story about how he'd "shot the same duck twice" after the wounded bird had regained consciousness in the back of his blind and scrambled toward the water in a futile escape attempt. ("He was, like, five feet in the air when I shot him again!") Displays feature what might strike nonhunters as a macabre array of bird and animal parts, including a selection of pelts and more than a dozen wings from various waterfowl species on a table with a sign that asks, "What Duck Am I? Feel Free to Touch!" At another table, an aproned wood carver from the Pacific Flyway Decoy Association whittles the head of a decoy eventually intended to lure unsuspecting waterfowl into a shot-gun's range.

The few early visitors enter past a plaque that honors Brower—the first executive director of the Sierra Club, as well as founder of Friends of the Earth, the League of Conservation Voters, and the Earth Island Institute—as "a fearless and indefatigable fighter for the Earth." To some it might seem incongruous for hunters to gather not just in conservation-minded Berkeley but in this particular building, where composting bins sit alongside the trash cans and the toilets offer a half-flush option.

And yet, despite the pre-event publicity and the *Chronicle*'s forecast of trouble, no protesters show. The rest of the world is aggressively ignoring the Federal Duck Stamp Contest, as usual. And although in the grand scheme, an art contest pales in sig-nificance compared to the unfolding disaster in the Gulf of Mexico, which for months has been the focus of attention among those involved in wildlife conservation, the contest organizers seem a little disappointed by the turnout to see the displayed 2010 entries and watch the judging.

Still, there's no shortage of drama. U.S. Fish and Wildlife Service staffers and volunteers busy themselves making sure the contest's carefully crafted choreography is ready to be set in motion. The communications coordinator from the Division of Bird Habitat Conservation is at her laptop, preparing the news release that will announce this year's winner. The program staffer who's been tweeting news about the event in recent days attends to final setup details. The five judges—whose identities have been a tightly controlled secret until today—are seques-tered in a second-floor briefing room, along with the Fish and Wildlife biologist who will act as their technical consultant once their deliberations begin. The AV guy is readying the camera for the first-ever worldwide webcast of the contest via live streaming video. Everyone entering the Brower Center this October weekend is greeted by a slotted box at the reception table. After viewing the displayed entries, visitors are invited to write their guess about the probable winner on a piece of paper and drop it into the box for a chance to win a rockin' pair of field binoculars. The voting table is crowded.

And of course, there are wildlife artists. Perhaps a dozen of the 235 contestants from around the country have come to witness the fate of their entry. Before the August 15 entry deadline, they had been at their easels—some of them for months— painting, in remarkably creative variations, the five duck and goose species declared eligible this year. Many of the artists have been competing against one another for years in the insular and sometimes quirky world of national pro-am duck painting— what one observer called "a strange, strange little backwater of the art industry"—and they're greeting one another with the energetic handshakes and lingering hugs of old friends who share a common passion.

Adam Nisbett, just twenty-three and working on a master's degree in electrical engineering, traveled all the way from his Missouri home to see how his painting of a single brant goose would fare. Robert Steiner, one of only two California artists to have won the prestigious federal contest in previous years, came across San Francisco Bay to watch his painting of a ruddy duck compete. Sherrie Russell Meline, the other California winner and one of only two women to have ever held the official title Federal Duck Stamp Artist, drove from Mount Shasta, hoping her Canada goose might prevail. Aerospace engineer

Mark Berger, who'd battled intense back pain during the 120 hours he'd spent painting his pair of flying Canada geese, drove up from his home south of Los Angeles. The reigning title-holder, Robert Bealle, flew in from Maryland. He's here for the presentation of his official prize—a framed pane of twenty stamps made from his 2009 winning painting, signed by Interior Secretary Ken Salazar—and to watch the selection of his successor. He has no horse in the 2010 race; contest rules prevent him from competing again for three years after his victory.

There's also a palpable pre-judging buzz about Minnesota's fabled Hautman brothers, whom Berger has described as "the New York Yankees of the Federal Duck Stamp Contest." Like Bealle, three-time winner Joe Hautman is sitting it out; his duck graced the 2008–2009 stamp, and he's ineligible to compete again until the 2011 contest. But his brothers Jim and Robert have entered paintings this year. Combined, the three brothers (whose family name is pronounced HAWT-man) have won the title an astounding eight times since 1989, and at least one of them has been among the top three finishers sixteen out of the previous twenty-two years. Will the rock stars of wildlife art actually show?

Adding to the Hautman buzz is the usual pre-contest handicapping, which has been going on for weeks. The paintings are judged anonymously, and officials of the Duck Stamp Program keep the artists' names a secret from the judges and the public until the winner has been chosen. But as it does each year, the program has posted scanned images of each 2010 entry on a program-affiliated website, OutdoorsWeekly.com. As usual, this has set off a whirlwind of speculation about the submitted works. Which of the five eligible species has predominated this year? Which paintings look familiar, either as previous entries or as derivative echoes of past entries? Which artists took smart risks? Which took less smart ones? And of course, which paintings are by the Hautmans?

Patricia—or Pat—Fisher has arrived from the Duck Stamp Program's Arlington headquarters. She watches the scene unfold with the detached air of someone who has seen it all before. Fisher professes not to care who wins, only that the contest is run with an integrity that honors its important mission, and the memory of those who in 1934 created what she and many others consider the greatest conservation program in history. The towering "Celebrate the Art of Conservation" poster is in place in the lobby. A Fish and Wildlife worker from the Pacific Southwest region, which is hosting the event, wanders through the crowd dressed as Puddles, the service's blue goose mascot.

Fisher watches Puddles take an awkward bow. "Every region has a Puddles costume," she says. "You have to have an outgoing personality to do that. Or really want a promotion."

As the clock nears ten A.M., the announced start time for opening remarks, Duck Stamp Program, Fish and Wildlife, and Department of the Interior officials; artists; and other visitors filter away from displays set up by seemingly disparate organizations, including the California Waterfowl Association ("Hunting for a Better California") and Audubon California ("Birds Matter"), and file into the reverentially dark auditorium. There's an unmistakable sense of anticipation in the air, a feeling that something important is about to happen. The artists know all too well the enormity of the stakes, at least in terms of their careers. For

wildlife conservation organizations struggling to preserve wetlands and other critical habitat in the face of forces as formidable
as land development and climate change, the stakes are even
higher.

But this year in particular there's an added layer of tension in
the room. Even as the auditorium doors close and the five judges
take their seats beneath the giant screen where their judgments
soon will be projected, those most familiar with the Duck
Stamp Program know that its future is suspended, for the moment, in a precarious balance.

The obscure drama of the Federal Duck Stamp Contest has
played out for more than six decades now, ever since the U.S.
Fish and Wildlife Service decided that its duck stamp painting
would no longer be an invitation-only commission offered to
chosen wildlife artists. The 1949 contest began the tradition of
an annual competition open to anybody with a paintbrush, the
entry fee, and a burning ambition to become the Federal Duck
Stamp Artist.[3]

In establishing the Duck Stamp Program, its organizers created an approach to conservation that in 2010 was being emu-
lated in thirty-four U.S. states with their own duck stamp or
other wildlife art program, as well as around the world. A
similar program was launched in 1946 by the Canadian prov-
ince of British Columbia, and by the late 1990s government
duck stamp programs had been launched in countries as diverse
as Australia, Russia, the United Kingdom, Iceland, Costa Rica,
Venezuela, Mexico, New Zealand, Belgium, Argentina, Den-
mark, Israel, Spain, Sweden, Ireland, Croatia, and Italy.[4] The
Federal Duck Stamp Contest—the only juried art competition

run by the U.S. government—created the improbable enterprise of competitive waterfowl painting, perhaps the narrowest niche in the known art world.

There's a Zen-garden quality to the whole enterprise, with the artists each year working within a rigid framework of contest rules that dictate everything from the year's eligible species, to the seven-by-ten-inch size and type of painting surface to the appropriate seasonal foliage and plumage that can appear in the painting. Winning entries have featured standing birds, sitting birds, swimming birds, flying birds, fall plumage, spring plumage, birds alone or in pairs or with hatchlings, birds taking off, birds landing, and once, on the now-legendary 1959–1960 stamp, even a limp mallard in the mouth of a national champion Labrador retriever named King Buck.

Deviations outside the contest's norms do happen—among the 2010 entries displayed in the Brower Center lobby, for example, is a painting that shows two Canada geese in flight against a backdrop of the blast plume from a space shuttle liftoff—but they seldom fare well. When they do, there's almost always controversy, such as with an entry one year that was not a painting of a duck at all, but a painting of a canvasback decoy. Had it not actually won the contest, that artistic anomaly might have passed unnoticed into the long and storied history of the Federal Duck Stamp Contest. But the judging decision that gave it the victory prompted much hand-wringing and eventually a rule change that required all future entries to feature an actual bird.

All this drama has unfolded far off the cultural radar screen. Although many hunters and conservationists and some birdwatchers know about the Federal Duck Stamp Program, other than that only wildlife artists and fans of filmmakers Joel and

Ethan Coen are likely to have heard of it and its annual Duck Stamp Contest. Even though by October 2010 the contest had been around for sixty-two years, and even though it has become what one recent news story called "the Academy Awards of wildlife stamp art,"[5] it has, in terms of public awareness, fallen somewhere between competitive bird-watching and lawn mower racing.

"You'd figure that if the federal government was going to have one juried art competition, it'd come out of the National Endowment for the Arts, not Fish and Wildlife," says program chief Fisher. "But there we are."

The Federal Duck Stamp has nothing to do with postage, even though many people buy duck stamps at their local post office. That misconception was created, in part, by the Coen brothers' 1996 film *Fargo*, which features a subplot revolving around Norm Gunderson, the husband of pregnant police chief Marge Gunderson, and his entry in that year's Federal Duck Stamp Contest. In the movie's final scene, Norm quietly announces that his mallard painting has been chosen for a three-cent postage stamp, while an unnamed Hautman's painting of a blue-winged teal will grace the more prestigious first-class stamp.

Actually, the Federal Duck Stamp is the revenue stamp that since 1934 all American waterfowl hunters over the age of sixteen have been required to buy and carry. In recent years about a million and a half hunters, conservationists, and collectors annually have paid for a duck stamp, which in 2010 cost fifteen dollars. For that price, not only are they federally certified to hunt, but the duck stamp also entitles them to free admission into all 553 national wildlife refuges.[6] Since the passage of the

1934 Migratory Bird Hunting Stamp Act, signed into law by President Franklin Roosevelt, ninety-eight cents of every dollar spent on the stamps has gone to the Migratory Bird Conservation Fund, the Small Wetlands Acquisition Program, and related reserves to buy and lease wetlands and other habitat for inclusion in the 150-million-acre National Wildlife Refuge System, which protects those resources for future generations. By 2010, the amount raised from duck stamp receipts, import duties on arms and ammunition, and other revenue sources was more than a billion dollars,[7] money that has been used to preserve 5.3 million acres—an area roughly the size of Vermont.

Without those preserves, commercial hunters and profiteers with increasingly efficient killing methods would have continued to decimate America's waterfowl populations, as they did through most of the eighteenth and nineteenth centuries, often for such frivolous reasons as the Victorian-era demand for ladies' hats festooned with the brightly colored plumes of various species. (Wrote one disgusted Chicago reporter, "It will be no surprise to me to see life-sized turkeys or even . . . farmyard hens on fashionable bonnets before I die.")[8] Since 1989, the U.S. government also has run the Junior Duck Stamp Contest, designed to build conservation awareness in a nation of youth drifting away from the natural world. A Fish and Wildlife Service brochure boasts, "Little wonder the Federal Duck Stamp Program has been called one of the most successful conservation programs ever initiated."

For both professional and amateur wildlife artists, the Federal Duck Stamp Contest is a chance to claim a measure of artistic immortality. In 1966, organizers began staging the judging process as a public event, at which point the competition moved into an entirely new phase.

"I call it America's first reality show," says Fisher. "*American Idol* for wildlife artists."

Fisher's comparison isn't just hyperbole. The judges are drawn mostly from the worlds of wildlife art and conservation, but participants recall a smattering of celebrity judges over the years. The program's efforts to add pizzazz to the proceedings by recruiting celebrity judges between 1994 and 2007 led to stints by actor Gary Burghoff (1993), who played Corporal Radar O'Reilly on the TV show *M\*A\*S\*H*; Dave Butz (1994), who in the 1980s had captained two Washington Redskins teams to Super Bowl victories; and Academy Award–nominated actress Jane Alexander (1995), who at the time was President Bill Clinton's appointee as chair of the National Endowment for the Arts. Other celebrity forays brought in former Cincinnati Reds pitcher and world-renowned duck decoy carver Jim Sprankle (twice, in 1998 and 2007) and Ward Burton (2005), who some-how juggles seemingly contradictory identities as both a re-spected environmentalist and a NASCAR driver.

The only celebrity the Duck Stamp Program could manage in 2009 was former Maryland congressman Wayne Gilchrest, a moderate Republican conservationist who had lost his seat the previous year. By 2010, Fisher had concluded that the whole celebrity-judge thing was misguided. "Celebrities don't do us any good because we can't use their names [to generate public-ity] in advance of the contest. So we've decided just to have the most qualified judging panels we can get."

Still, as on *Idol*, the buildup to the two-day, three-round judging process can be thrilling, or devastating. In the tight-

knit, insular world of duck stamp obsessives, pre-contest handicapping is as much a part of the competition as the paintings
themselves. As the judging weekend approaches, handicapping
unfolds in private conversations, on Internet message boards, in
Facebook postings, and in gallery gossip sessions. Almost all of
it is pointless, of course, since no one knows what the judges
want, or even who they are. But that doesn't stop artists and
collectors from pursuing their guesswork with the zeal of research scientists.

Many contestants have been competing for the Federal Duck
Stamp Artist title—and against one another—for decades, and
they're all too familiar with the harsh finality of the contest's
first cull. In it, the judges simply vote the painting "In" or
"Out," with three "In" votes needed to move on to the second
round. During the 2009-contest judging—which was held at
the Patuxent Research Refuge, near Laurel, Maryland—
competitors, conservationists, and wildlife-art aficionados gathered in a similarly darkened auditorium as a heavy tension
settled over the room. The first-round tallies were flashed onto
a giant screen behind the judges.

When all five judges voted a painting out, everyone in the
room saw the 5–0 rebuke. The year before, recalls one California competitor, one artist burst into tears after failing to make
the first cut.

Still, the annual Federal Duck Stamp Contest is one of the
biggest and most influential events in the world of conservation, and it has lured generations of artists into the world of wildlife painting. It also has scared a few away.

"Since I was a little fledgling bird artist, maybe fourteen
years old or so, friends were urging me to do the duck stamp

thing," recalls David Allen Sibley, author and illustrator of many landmark birding books, including *The Sibley Guide to Birds*, considered by many bird enthusiasts to be the most comprehensive guide for North American field identification. "They said, 'You've gotta do this! It's worth millions! You'll be set for life if you win it once! The duck stamp is where it's at!' But I've never entered. It wasn't really my thing, and I never got around to getting the entry form and getting organized to be able to enter."

But, Sibley concedes, it was more than that. "My reluctance to enter was partly because, whenever I looked into it a little bit, I saw how competitive it was. And there are these brothers who win it year after year. So I felt it wasn't really my strength, and I didn't feel like I'd have much chance of winning."

It's a startling revelation, considering Sibley's lofty place in the world of wildlife art. But his reluctance underscores just how deep the rabbit hole goes. Delve far enough into this peculiar American subculture, and you'll find a fascinating cast of characters arrayed on a stage where legends have been born, dreams have died, and controversies have flared. Critics are still upset about the year the winning painting depicted a duck with an incorrect number of flight feathers, allegedly because the artist had used a photograph of a pen-kept duck with clipped wings as his model. (The painting was not disqualified, simply amended before it was turned into a stamp. But around that time, organizers began making sure a biologist was available as a technical adviser during the judging process.) And grumbling continues about the Federal Duck Stamp Contest winner who was accused of using a stencil to make supposedly freehand remarques—small, personalized drawings on a print, usually near the artist's signature, meant to increase value—on prints of his winning painting, essentially mass-producing what should have been unique drawings.

The temptation of money sometimes trumps artistic integrity, of course, and temptation abounds when the title Federal Duck Stamp Artist is at stake. Says Robert Richert, a California landscape artist who has entered the contest almost every year since 1979 and who won his state's competition in 1982, "The national recognition overnight can be worth its weight in gold."

That keys neatly into an enduring American fascination with the idea that ordinary people, through hard work and talent, can completely change their lives. The Fish and Wildlife Service expends considerable energy stoking such dreams. While the contest offers no cash prize or direct income to the winning artist—winners receive only that framed pane of twenty duck stamps featuring their painting—a brochure notes, "The wildlife artist who wins this competition knows that his or her career and fortunes will take wing!"

The reason: The top-scoring entries are "enthusiastically exhibited" around the country at museums, festivals, and expositions, and those events are always a big draw for both collectors and wildlife-art enthusiasts. From an artist's point of view, the tour and the stamp are preposterously visible government-subsidized advertisements for the original painting—to which the artist retains all rights—as well as for the artist's other work. A lot of hunters, conservationists, ornithologists, and collectors want to own a limited-edition print of the image that's on the Federal Duck Stamp, or at least some other piece of the artist's work, and the artist can sell as many prints as the market will bear. Licensing deals for the winning artist's work mean it can turn up on just about anything—calendars, rugs, umbrellas, wallpaper, clocks, hats, lawn chairs, one-thousand-piece jigsaw puzzles, shower curtains, Christmas stockings, tree ornaments, even toilet seats.

At times in the past, winning artists have made more than a million dollars in sales and licensing fees, which is why many still refer to the painting as "the million-dollar duck." One winner is said to have made more than twice that.

While the spoils these days are more modest, between 200 and 250 artists each year still embark on a quest to overcome obscurity, achieve instant wealth, and secure their place in the pantheon of notable American wildlife artists. The contest has attracted the most diverse and sometimes eccentric collection of artists imaginable; winners have included physicists, scholars, engineers, housewives, commercial designers, cartoonists, photographers, and, in 1988, a guy who during a previous career had won both the Best Chest and the Most Muscular trophies in the Mr. Minnesota bodybuilding contest.[9] In a sense, the Federal Duck Stamp Contest is a pure and abiding expression of the American dream.

# THE FIRST BATTLE OF
# SPECKLEBELLY

I N  M A Y  2 0 1 0, three months before the August 15 Federal
Duck Stamp Contest deadline, Jim Hautman is getting ready
to leave his Minnesota River bluffs home in Chaska, just outside
Minneapolis, on a photographic expedition to a family friend's
farm in New Germany, Minnesota, a small rural outpost less
than an hour away. This is not a pleasure trip; this is business.

By his own estimate, the three-time Federal Duck Stamp
Contest winner already has about seventy thousand reference
photos of waterfowl and other wildlife in his collection. They
overflow the tabletops and shelves of his home studio, where
both a computer-controlled treadmill and a Stickley-style easy
chair look out on a stunning woodland vista that tumbles down
a valley toward the town of Shakopee. Hautman is a constant
student of birds. That easy chair, for instance, sits on a small
wooden platform in front of the studio's wraparound picture
windows like the captain's chair on the Starship *Enterprise*. Just
off its right arm sits a pair of binoculars and a hardbound copy
of the book *Painting Wildlife with John Seerey-Lester*. The chair
and the treadmill are the only real points of order in the room;

the rest of the space is like an open and unruly file cabinet that's roamed freely by Hautman's house cat, Bradley.

Shelves are jammed with taxidermied birds, dried bird parts, and boxes with cryptic markings—"Leaves," "Turkey," "Alaska." Hautman stores the slides of birds he photographed in the early 1980s in transparent sleeves, but he grew tired of squinting at them for the details he needed to transform those reference photos into paintings. He began developing his pictures as prints in the 1990s, and he still keeps those in tattered cardboard boxes around the studio, cataloging them according to a system of his own design. Even after he switched to more efficient digital photography around 2000, his system of tracking his pictures only seemed to grow more unwieldy.

"Cataloging them, that's a tough one," he says. As he speaks, a cocky wild turkey saunters past the studio's windows. "It keeps branching out. First you have a 'Duck' file with a couple hundred ducks in it. Then you start breaking them down into species. Then maybe after a while you've got two thousand mallard photos. Then you break them down into swimming, standing, flying. And 'Scene' is kind of the same thing. You have 'Northern Scene,' and 'Winter Scene,' and pretty soon you've got fifty different categories, you know? And it's hard to decide which one to put them in sometimes. It's real frustrating when you can't find a picture. Sometimes you'll have a photo clear in your mind, the right photo you need for some detail of a painting, and you can't find it. It drives you crazy."

Even with an extensive library of semi-organized images, Jim Hautman is on a very specific mission as he leaves for the farm in New Germany. He has already won the federal contest multiple times, his first victory coming in 1989. But his last win was in 1998. He's certainly been a fierce competitor since then, with three of his four second-place finishes coming in 2003, 2004, and 2008. But for twelve years, someone else's painting has been on the stamp. To Jim Hautman, that has felt like a long, long drought. Plus, three times during those twelve years, the bird on the stamp had been painted by one of his older brothers, Robert (or Bob) and Joe.

He applauds their successes, of course, but theirs is a sibling rivalry like no other.

"You're just trying to win, you're trying to beat everybody," he says. "And that includes *everybody*. If you don't win, you hope your brother wins, or you hope your friends win. But you have to beat everybody to win. So Bob, Joe, and I just look at each other as, you know . . ."

Hautman pauses to choose his next words carefully: "As the biggest threats, actually."

As he sets out for his May 2010 photo recon mission, Jim Hautman knows it's way past time to get back in the game.

Each year, the organizers of the Federal Duck Stamp Program consult their list of forty-two eligible North American waterfowl species and decide which sets of five will be the focus of future contests.[1] This is something that they and aspiring competitors take seriously, so seriously that by the spring of 2010 the selections had been made—and made public—through the year 2016. Each year's eligible species are drawn from nine categories that include not only diving and dabbling ducks but also whistling ducks, swans, geese, sea ducks, mergansers, and stiff-tailed ducks, and the list includes such prosaic species names as the black-bellied whistling duck, the spectacled eider, and the bufflehead.

For the 2010 contest, the organizers chose the brant, the northern shoveler, the ruddy duck, the Canada goose, and the white-fronted goose, also known as the specklebelly goose. Since the brant is actually a small goose, three of the five species eligible for the 2010 Federal Duck Stamp Contest are not, technically, ducks.

For the job of introducing the eligible species for 2010 in this book, I contact John Solberg, an avuncular North Dakota pilot and biologist for the U.S. Fish and Wildlife Service's Division of Migratory Bird Management, who is a candidate to serve as the technical expert for the upcoming Duck Stamp Contest finals in October. (In the summer of 2010, Soberg would decide to retire.)

## The Brant

A smallish goose that prefers brackish waters, this short-billed, mostly black bird is like a feathered Martha Stewart. "They build beautiful nests," Solberg says. "They probably put more down in their nests [for insulation] than any other waterfowl." They also make incredibly long flights during their migration. "They'll leave Izembek Lagoon in Alaska [where they gorge on eelgrass while getting ready to migrate] and show up on the Washington or Oregon coast, and it's thought they make that voyage in a single flight."

That could be one thousand miles nonstop before they land, rest, and continue on toward major West Coast lagoons and Mexico's Baja peninsula. Brant, which tend to dabble on top of the water rather than dive into it, migrate in smaller flocks than other goose species, and they fly low, like the rogue American bomber in *Dr. Strangelove*. "They may be ten to twenty feet off the water the whole trip," Solberg says. One birding guide characterizes their call as a low, hoarse "cronk,"[2] which sounds remarkably unattractive.

To a painter, brant are distressingly monochromatic. Granted, that makes painting them a bit easier. Plus, the males and females look pretty much alike, which means artists who typically choose to represent one bird of each gender can get away with painting only one brant instead of a pair. But it's hard to find an artist who's excited about the prospect of painting the small goose, except perhaps those competitors whose futile pre-contest handicapping convinces them that the brant is appealing simply *because* no one else wants to paint one.

### The Northern Shoveler

Think of this dabbling duck as the Lady Gaga of the wetlands. Solberg calls it "the Hollywood mallard," citing its iridescent green head and neck and its "extremely showy plumage," including a white chest and breast and a chestnut belly and sides. A white stripe extends from the breast along the margin of the gray-brown back, and the wings have a gray-blue shoulder patch separated from a bright green speculum by a tapered white stripe.[3]

But then there's that Jimmy Durante schnoz; the bird is called a shoveler because its spoon-shaped bill is narrow at the base, just below its bright yellow eyes, and widens and flattens toward the tip. (Using a particularly evocative ornithological term, Solberg calls it a "spatulate" bill.) The tip is so large and flat that Solberg wonders if the northern shoveler's characteristic dipped-head position in flight is the result of wind resistance.

But what looks like a practical joke actually is a feeding

adaptation. As they dabble along the water's surface, often cir-
cling in groups to help stir up invertebrates and plant parts,
shovelers dip their bills and filter water and food through a
comblike feature inside the bill that's much like baleen on a
whale. Sometimes a shoveler will swim forward with its head
partly underwater, eating larger prey as it moves. Matching the
shoveler's anatomical goofiness is its unfortunate call, which one
online bird-identification site describes as a "repeated, liquid,
hollow g-dunk, g-dunk, g-dunk,"[4] at least among males trying
to show off.

### The Ruddy Duck

"Kind of an oddball," Solberg says, because its sky blue bill is
just flat-out ridiculous, although Solberg prefers the term "highly
unique." The ruddy was the only stiff-tailed duck selected as an
eligible species for the 2010 contest. Those tail feathers stick up
sharply, like thrust deflectors at the end of an airport runway.
Fed by blood from a large center vein that runs the length of
each, the feathers are similar to the goose feathers that made
terrific quill pens back in pre-ballpoint days. When still attached to the duck, they make even better rudders in both the air
and the water. In males, the distinctive upthrust tail looks like a
sort of ass-end pompadour, which, along with what Solberg
calls a "very showy display," signals to potential mates, "That's
right, I'm your species. How *you* doin'?"

The ruddy is a diving duck—as opposed to a surface-dwelling
dabbling duck—that prefers food found deep beneath the surface of a pond, lake, or marsh. Ruddies can easily dive down
between three and ten feet, moving as if flying underwater.
Their bodies have evolved in ways that make them much like

seals, which have more hemoglobin in their blood and tissue to carry more oxygen, enabling them to stay underwater longer. One reason diving ducks are less buoyant in the water is that their bones have thicker walls and therefore are heavier than those of dabbling ducks, which are more like bobbing corks as they feed mostly on the surface or just beneath the surface. (They're the ones that tip their feathered rumps to the sky while foraging underwater.) Also, the position of a diving duck's legs makes it better suited for underwater propulsion than for flight. When scared, ruddies are more likely to plunge deep into a pond or marsh than they are to fly away.

As part of the species's mating ritual, a ruddy male on the make bobs his head and makes a "chuck-uck-uck-uck-ur-r-r"[5] sound, but the female ruddy is mostly silent. This is different than in most duck species, Solberg says, noting that most artificial duck calls, like the ones hunters pay a hundred dollars or more for at their local Bass Pro or Cabela's outfitter, are designed to emulate the sound of the females, since they're generally more vocal than the males.

Speaking of female ruddy ducks, a moment of respectful silence, please. "In proportion to their body size," Solberg notes, "they may lay the largest egg of all the duck species. It's a huge egg for one of our smallest ducks, as big as the egg laid by a wild turkey." Plus, he says, the gray-white surface of the shell is "granular and real rough." Female ruddy ducks also have a keen instinct for propelling their species forward. Knowing that it's hard to warm and protect a clutch of those titanic eggs with their small bodies, they'll sometimes lay them in the nests of other waterfowl, hoping to cadge a little free incubation work from unsuspecting mothers.

### The Canada Goose

Hunted to near extinction in the early 1900s, this notorious honker—now with about a dozen recognized sub-races—has rebounded with a vengeance, so much so that in July 2010 federal wildlife officials rounded up hundreds of them at the placid lake in Brooklyn's Prospect Park and took them away to be gassed. (This sad state of affairs followed an incident in January 2009 in which Canada geese were sucked into the engines of US Airways Flight 1549 minutes after the plane took off from LaGuardia Airport, forcing the pilots to land in the Hudson River. The incident made a hero out of Captain Chesley "Sully" Sullenberger III and a scapegoat out of the geese.) Their population in the Mississippi Flyway increased by an average of 3 percent a year from 1998 to 2007, when, according to the private conservation organization Ducks Unlimited, it was estimated at more than 1.6 million birds. Some studies suggest that there are now more than 3 million nationwide, and several states have begun similar goose culls or decided to start their goose-hunting season early to help reduce the geese's numbers.[6] One reason they're proliferating is that the Canada goose seems just as comfortable in an urban park as it does in arctic solitude; Solberg says it's probably the most recognized waterfowl species in the United States.

Another reason may be that Canada geese are the Ozzie and Harriet of the migratory-waterfowl kingdom. Once a male and female bond, they stick together for a long time, if not for life—a proclivity for pair bonding that makes most duck species look downright promiscuous by comparison. Plus, Solberg says, "they're extremely good parents, very attentive to their offspring," and don't seem to mind human activity in their breeding areas. Some artists, including Southern California–based Duck Stamp Contest competitor Mark Berger, say that those characteristics make Canada geese particularly attractive as subjects, because they work not only as wildlife art but also as a symbol of fidelity and family.

Others just find them beautiful, with their black heads, cheek-to-cheek white bands that look like chin straps, wide and graceful wings, and plump bodies (Solberg says that males of the "giant" type can reach twenty pounds) that range in color from light gray to a dark chocolate brown. "They're my favorite birds," says artist Sherrie Russell Meline, who in 2006 became the second woman to win the federal contest, with a painting of a Ross's goose. "I don't know why, but there's just something soft and regal about them."

Of course, that observation requires overlooking their somewhat less regal personal habits. Their familiar "Aah! Aah!"[7] call is a nasal honk that brings to mind TV sitcom actress Fran Drescher. You find a lot of them hanging around golf courses like entitled trust-funders, dabbling in the water hazards and relieving themselves at the water's edge, making ball retrieval and shots from the drop zones a sometimes messy, unpleasant affair.

In the peculiar calculus of a competing duck stamp artist, Meline is thinking about how potential judges might regard the Canada goose as she weighs her options for 2010. "People that live on a golf course probably hate 'em," she says. "They mess up the lawns. There's tons of geese that come into some of the parks and make the parks unwalkable at certain times of the year. But you know what? It doesn't matter. To me they're still the best, and that's why I'll paint one this year."

## The Specklebelly (or White-Fronted) Goose

Solberg calls them "beautiful," but the deconstructed specklebelly—officially known as the white-fronted goose—sounds like a collection of spare parts: brownish gray head, orange or pinkish bill surrounded by a wide halo of white feathers (thus the "white-fronted" descriptor), and bright orange legs and feet. Its chest plumage is grayish brown when it's young, but in adults it turns whitish with rich black bars running horizontally across the breast. Some look like they belly flopped onto a patch of wet paint—thus the nickname.

They're small compared to the Canada goose—the largest males reach only 6.2 pounds—but they share with that species a tendency toward strong pair bonds, a habit of chattering, and a preference for privacy. Even their flocks are small, often between five and seven birds. When nesting, the pairs sometimes put a mile of tundra between themselves and others. (Snow geese, by contrast, prefer the waterfowl equivalent of housing tracts, with as many as fifty thousand nesting in a square mile.) When around water, they mostly dabble and feed on marsh grasses, aquatic plants, and insects, but they also work farm fields and sedges for grains and berries. In recordings, their high-pitched "Uh-uh! Uh-uh!" squeaking sounds like the chirp of Air Jordans on a wooden court during a pickup basketball game.[8]

By the time he arrives in New Germany, Jim Hautman has limited his options for his contest painting to two of 2010's five eligible species, the northern shoveler and the specklebelly goose.

Hautman suspects that a lot of artists will paint the Canada goose this year. "The judges can get pretty burned out if they see too many of one species. Sometimes it takes something different to wake them up."

He decides against the brant because "they're not real popular, plus they're plain brown-and-black birds."

As for the ruddy duck, "I knew I didn't want to paint a bird on the water, which would be the best way to paint a ruddy duck. They're awkward-looking to me when they're standing or flying."

According to those who know him best, this decision-making process is typical of Jim Hautman. Oldest brother Pete, a fifty-seven-year-old writer, says that Jim is his family's best poker player—analytical, disciplined, a consistent winner. As a child, and the youngest of seven siblings, Jim idolized his analytical older brother Joe. And as an adult, Pete says, "Jim is always focused and methodical in everything he does in his life," an approach that serves him well in the business of art.

"When he's doing a painting," says Pete, "he knows what he wants to do, who it's for, and how it fits into his business . . . Jim's is a very scientific approach. He's a planner. He has tremendous focus. You can feel that in his paintings. They exude confidence. He knows what he wants to do, and he does it."

Joe, Jim, and Bob Hautman all accept commissions, and they license their work—a key part of their considerable incomes. But Pete says that Jim is the one who probably makes the most money. "If their licensing agent says roseate spoonbills are going to be big this year because they were featured in some fashion shoot or whatever, Jim is the one who's likely to produce several paintings in response to that perceived need," he says. "Bob and Joe might do it, but they'd do it grudgingly. The whole concept of the scientific method, the pragmatic part of it, the demonstrate-it-to-me-first-before-I-believe thing—Jim really embraced that."

At his friend's farm, Jim finds both shovelers and captive specklebellies, but he already is leaning toward specklebellies. Every Duck Stamp Contest artist engages in the often pointless calculus of guessing what might impress the unknown judges. Artists also consult their available reference photographs and try to guess which species will best suit their painting style to give themselves the best odds of winning. But the Hautmans seem better than most at this guessing game.

The 2010 judging is going to be held in California for the first time ever, and Jim figures it's a safe bet that there will be a Western skew to the panel. And he knows, as do many competitors, that the specklebelly goose is a familiar presence in parts of the American West. When it's time for them to head south from their summertime nesting areas near the Arctic Circle from Alaska to central Canada, a lot of specklebellies migrate along the Pacific or Central flyways and winter in California's Central Valley, as well as in coastal and central regions of Mexico, Arkansas, and coastal Texas and Louisiana.

Western judges. Western bird. To Jim Hautman, the specklebelly seems like a logical choice. Hautman even knows the pose he wants: two birds, a goose and a gander, standing side by side.

He rules out the shoveler, thinking that it poses potential problems. He's not concerned about the bird's plumage; it's spectacular. Nor is he worried because its bill has a weirdly comical shape. He rules it out for a seemingly bizarre reason: Some hunters don't like the way it tastes. "There's almost a prejudice against them," he says. "That could be a factor."

But now he needs reference photos, lots of them, because the

Minnesota native is less familiar with the primarily Western goose than with other ducks and geese on the eligible-species list. Hautman wants to get to know his subjects. He needs more than just photographs of specklebellies from every possible angle, in every possible light. He needs to *be* the specklebelly, and he hopes he'll find the specklebelly soul among the captive birds at the farm in New Germany.

By the time he's done shooting pictures, Hautman is sure he has made the right choice: "Just hanging out in the same pen with them for a couple of days helped. To be able to see their mannerisms and the differences between individuals was pretty cool."

At this point, the three-time winner is fully committed, specklebellies or bust. Plus, he has another twenty-five hundred photographs to add to his collection.

Given his businesslike approach to art, it's surprising to hear Jim Hautman describe the creation of his 2010 specklebelly entry as "a battle." After his photo marathon at the farm in New Germany, he sets about finally putting brush to canvas and begins to mull over other choices yet to be made. He has noticed an apparent preference among recent judges for simpler designs— the top three picks in 2009 were all birds on the water with almost no background at all—and his goal is "to have enough going on in the painting, but still have it appear as a simple design."

But that's when things get complicated.

In his home studio, Hautman creates a small, full-color study of the painting, just two by three inches, to try out background colors. He starts with a design that's relatively monochromatic.

"Orangish light on the brown birds, with the sky sort of orangey too, with purplish clouds. It all kind of worked."

Then he translates that study into a full-size painting. His first pass at the two standing birds looks good, he decides. But to his artist's eye, there's something unsettling about the background and sky based on his original orange-tinged concept. It's not working.

The indecision and struggle are disorienting to someone so accustomed to a methodical approach. Fighting off his reluctance to reimagine the piece, Hautman decides on a different background, which soon becomes "the battle of the whole painting." He tries blue sky and thunderheads, but quickly concludes that's not working either. He tries including a lake, then takes the lake out. Then he paints the lake back in. Finally, frustrated, he paints out the whole background with a flat gray color, intending to start over.

He stops. Something about that muted gray makes the colorful specklebellies pop off the surface. Hautman begins to paint the flat gray into some nimbus clouds that suggest a building storm. Suddenly, the painting exudes unmistakable energy, like a crackling electrical charge. Something dramatic seems to be taking place between the storm in the background and the birds in the foreground, which look like they're on high alert. It's more than just birds against a background scene. In the painting that has begun unfolding beneath Jim Hautman's brushes, a drama is taking shape involving two birds and an approaching storm.

As he paints, Hautman feels like a trapeze artist working without a net—and he finds it strangely exhilarating. "As soon as I did it, I was happy with it. And all that time, the birds just sort of sat there. There's probably eight coats of paint on the background, and one on the birds."

When he's done, Hautman asks his wife, Dorothy, for her assessment. She's more than simply a supportive spouse; the former Dorothy Deas has her own history with the Duck Stamp Program. In 1989, when Hautman won his first federal contest with a pair of flying black-bellied whistling ducks, the then-shy youngest member of the Hautman clan found himself flushed overnight from his idyllic rural life onto the national stage. Hautman was just twenty-five—at the time, the youngest winner in contest history. He'd been so shy as a kid that he "took Fs on a lot of oral book reports just to get out of having to stand up and speak . . . I was used to hanging out by myself in the studio and painting. Promoting myself was not something I was comfortable with. Being public was all new to me."

All during the post-victory celebration the night of the announcement, though, "the phone was ringing off the hook. People I'd known. Newspapers. Magazines. Radio shows. We just invited them all over for the party." Plus, back then winning the federal contest meant flying to Washington, D.C., to receive the personal congratulations of the president of the United States, who at the time was George H. W. Bush. For that and many other reasons, Hautman was nervous. "I'd traveled, but always with someone else on hunting or fishing trips. That was my first trip by myself."

He arrived at an airport in Washington—he doesn't remember which one, but it was what's now called Ronald Reagan Washington National Airport—with "an interesting feeling of anonymity." Bewildered by the big-city clamor, maybe a little hungover from the party the night before, he heard someone call his name. It was a pretty young brunette with a charming Southern accent, a special assistant to the director of the Fish and Wildlife Service, there to escort the winner on his rounds.

They married five years later.

Hautman waits as his toughest critic studies his 2010 painting. Typically, his wife is guarded. She's aware of how intensely competitive the contest can be, and that her husband's two brothers often represent his toughest opponents. But this time, for the first time in five years, she is unrestrained in her approval.

"You win," she says.

In late August, two weeks after sending his 2010 contest entry to the Duck Stamp Program's headquarters in Arlington, Jim Hautman is still feeling confident. Those standing specklebellies, he says, are "as good an entry as I've had."

## 3

## GUNS, GREED, AND
## THE GRAND IDEA

ALTHOUGH THE FEDERAL Duck Stamp Program was signed into law by President Franklin Roosevelt in 1934, its roots go far deeper. In fact, the program was a desperate reaction to a problem that had been gathering momentum since European settlers had first set foot on North American soil three centuries before—the strip-mining of the New World's wildlife.

The advance guard of European settlers arrived in what must have seemed like a fantasy, a seemingly endless smorgasbord of accessible protein, a shooting gallery of meat. The settlers had come from a heavily populated continent where humans already had made a sizable dent in the wildlife population. By the seventeenth and eighteenth centuries, subsistence in Europe meant hard work. But in the New World, settlers were surrounded by abundance. Wild turkeys, deer, beavers, and other game shared the forests; overflying ducks, geese, swans, quail, and pigeons darkened the skies; ponds, lakes, and rivers were glutted with fish.

A certain and unmistakable giddiness runs through settlers' early accounts. William Wood wrote in 1634's *New England's*

*Prospect*, "If I should tell you how some have killed a hundred geese in a week, fifty ducks at a shot, forty teals at another, it may be counted impossible though nothing more than certain."[1] Nearly four decades after Wood, in 1673, settler John Josselyn wrote a similar account: "I have seen a flight of pidgeons [*sic*] in the spring . . . for four or five miles that to my thinking had neither beginning nor ending, length or breadth, and so thick I could see no sun."[2]

For the most part, overhunting wasn't a problem in the days when most hunters were just trying to feed their families and were relying on inaccurate flintlock rifles to do so. Even without government regulation, the wholesale taking of wildlife was limited by all sorts of factors, including those balky rifles and the lack of refrigeration and transportation that would have made commercial hunting viable. Still, by the early 1700s, some New Worlders had begun to recognize a problem.

By 1708, certain counties in New York had instituted the first closed seasons on birds, protecting species such as grouse, quail, and turkeys. Two years later, Massachusetts prohibited the use of camouflaged canoes or sailboats in the pursuit of waterfowl.[3]

But of course, the settlers kept coming, and the newcomers had to eat. During the century between 1790 and 1890, the nation's population exploded from about four million to nearly sixty-three million.[4] During that same period, the railroads opened and began carrying more and more people from the eastern seaboard into the center of the continent, straight into the deeply imprinted flyways of migratory waterfowl. Back then, the resource seemed endless. But just as nature abhors a vacuum, a free market abhors natural resources with unrealized commercial potential. Some of those pioneers started coming up with better ways to hunt, and not just to feed their families. They were called "market hunters."

The arrival of the railroads in the early 1800s spurred the growth of new cities and towns, and the commercial market for ducks, geese, and other game birds got bigger. The advent of refrigerated boxcars in the middle of that century enabled market hunters to ship their birds far beyond the flyways where they were killed.

To meet the demand, the most enterprising hunters invented some remarkable weapons of mass destruction. Around 1820, they began replacing flintlocks with more reliable and accurate muzzle-loading percussion guns. Double-barreled models followed, which allowed a hunter to fire two rounds in quick succession before any unscathed birds could react to the first shot and flee. In short order, the weapons began morphing into sometimes absurd-looking but effective variations, including the twelve-foot-long punt gun, a sort of shotgun on steroids that was capable of launching a pound of shot from a fair distance across a pond into an unsuspecting flotilla of waterfowl, and the battery gun, which was a menacing array of gun barrels that protruded like quills from a boat's bow and could be fired simultaneously once the hunter had rowed quietly within range. In their book *The Duck Stamp Story*, authors Eric Jay Dolin and Bob Dumaine note that battery guns sometimes "malfunctioned, thereby reducing the population of market hunters one or two at a time."[5]

Those were small victories for the waterfowl, but by the late 1800s, a wide cultural schism had developed between hunters who considered themselves sportsmen and those who hunted the same game commercially. In the same way that a weekend marlin fisherman has nothing in common with a commercial drift net fishing operator that scours the ocean by scooping up any living thing in its wake, sport hunters had little in common with—and little respect for—mercenary market hunters. Sport hunters were frustrated because waterfowl, which tend to be cautious anyway, were growing increasingly wary. Maybe the widespread use of punt and battery guns had eroded their safety-in-numbers instincts, but the birds were now more likely to avoid situations where something seemed amiss, such as a sport hunter's decoys carefully arranged across the surface of a pond. Sport hunters began forming their own private clubs so they wouldn't have to share space with the market hunters, whom former president Grover Cleveland, a passionate hunter, once accused of "bald assassination" and "murder for the sake of money."[6]

Of course, waterfowl weren't the only casualties of the sometimes mindless wildlife carnage during the 1800s. The teeming herds of buffalo that once roamed the Great Plains—estimates range between thirty million and two hundred million of them between the Mississippi River and the Rocky Mountains[7]—were slaughtered by trappers, traders, and others among the wave of white settlers moving westward. While Native American tribes had developed nifty techniques for high-volume hunting, including the rather nasty process of stampeding the herds over cliffs in so-called buffalo jumps, they also were conscientious in their use of the meat, fur, and other buffalo by-products. By the 1870s, though, white trappers and traders were killing hundreds of thousands of buffalo each year and shipping their hides eastward, and most of the meat went to waste. According to the documentary film *American Buffalo: Spirit of a Nation*, aired as part of PBS's award-winning *Nature* program, more than a million and a half hides were packed aboard trains and wagons during the winter of 1872–1873 alone.[8]

The hunting habits of some newcomers to the West made old-fashioned waterfowl market hunters look downright moderate. "Train companies offered tourists the chance to shoot buffalo from the windows of their coaches, pausing only when they ran out of ammunition or the gun's barrel became too hot," writes David Malakoff in the online introduction to the PBS documentary. "There were even buffalo killing contests. In one, a Kansan set a record by killing 120 bison in just 40 minutes. 'Buffalo' Bill Cody, hired to slaughter the animals, killed more than 4,000 buffalo in just two years."

Some U.S. government officials even promoted the destruction of the buffalo herds as a way to defeat Native Americans resisting the U.S. settlement of the West. Malakoff recounts the words of Texas congressman James Throckmorton, who believed "it would be a great step forward in the civilization of the Indians and the preservation of peace on the border if there was not a buffalo in existence." Malakoff also writes that "one general believed that buffalo hunters 'did more to defeat the Indian nations in a few years than soldiers did in 50.'"

By 1880, fewer than two thousand of the animals remained in the United States, with the largest wild herd of a few hundred survivors sequestered in Yellowstone National Park, which had been created eight years earlier.

The parallel decimation of waterfowl also escalated through the 1800s, the slaughter fueled by hunger and a Victorian-era fashion that involved decorating hats and other headwear with bird parts—parts often taken by plume hunters during breeding season, when the birds' feathers were the most beautiful. Favorites included the plumage of snowy egrets, roseate spoonbills, scarlet ibis, and great white herons, and authors Dolin and Dumaine write that "some went so far as to have landscaped scenes atop their heads, replete with stuffed birds strutting about."

Plume hunting was so profitable during that era that about five million birds were being killed each year for fashion's sake, with one hunter setting a record by killing 141,000 birds in a single season. An ornithologist of the period did a walkabout survey on the streets of New York and found that 542 of the 700 women's hats he observed displayed parts of various birds.[9]

"There was a whole lot of 'We'll never run out of it' attitude in the 1800s," says Dale Hall, former director of the U.S. Fish and Wildlife Service and now CEO of Memphis-based Ducks Unlimited, which, with 650,000 members, is the world's largest private waterfowl-and-wetlands conservation organization, as well as a longtime ally of the Federal Duck Stamp Program. Hall's organization partners with the program and has helped conserve more than twelve million acres of waterfowl habitat in North America, and influenced through policy measures the conservation of another forty-eight million acres. "Commercial hunters were really doing some serious damage to the bird population," he says.

The backlash among conservationists and sport hunters was growing, however, built in part upon a foundation laid earlier in the century—by an artist.

In October 1820, failed businessman John James Audubon, along with Joseph Mason, his thirteen-year-old assistant, set out from Cincinnati with his gun and a paint box on a journey down the Ohio and Mississippi rivers to paint life-size portraits of all the bird species he could. He followed that muse down the Mississippi River to New Orleans, across the South into Florida, up the Atlantic Coast to Labrador, and through the Great Plains of the Dakotas. In those pre-photography days, and because his subjects so often were unwilling to pose, Audubon sometimes shot scores of birds to death for each painting, chose the most attractive specimens, then used wire to rig them into appealing poses.

By 1827, Audubon had completed his quest and raised enough money to begin publishing and selling *Birds of America*, a monumental book of prints featuring his paintings of 497 bird species. Many experts consider Audubon's book the big bang in the world of wildlife art. Made from engraved copperplates and published in seven volumes between 1827 and 1838, it's now considered one of the greatest picture books ever produced. A British lord put one of the 119 first editions known to exist up for auction in December 2010, and the successful bidder, sixty-six-year-old London art dealer Michael Tollemache, paid the equivalent of $11.5 million for it, making it the world's most expensive book.[10] (A similar edition of Audubon's masterwork had become the world's most expensive book a decade earlier after selling for about $8.8 million.)[11]

Audubon began using his paintings in illustrated guidebooks and selling those by subscription, and those guidebooks introduced the world to the beauty and variety of bird species that few had ever actually experienced firsthand. Even today, guidebooks inspired by Audubon's originals, along with audio recordings, remain the basic tool used by an estimated forty-eight million American bird-watchers, many of whom have made a sport of cataloging the species they have seen.

Audubon's work created an awareness of and appreciation for birds around the world, and coincided with the beginning of a new way of thinking about wildlife in the mid-nineteenth century, one that established the principle that wildlife resources are owned by no one and should be held in trust by the government for the benefit of future generations. It was a radical notion at the time, as controversial as the notion of climate change is today. Wildlife once seemed as infinite as the air around us, and recognizing its limits and urging responsibility for conserving a seemingly endless resource was not a great way to win friends.

But during the decades that followed the publication of *Birds of America*, something remarkable happened. In 1842, a U.S. Supreme Court ruling in a New Jersey oyster-harvesting rights case called *Martin v. Waddell*[12] laid the groundwork in U.S. common law for the principle that the American government should protect wildlife. Around the same time, officials in Canada began to take steps to prevent the kind of wildlife exploitation they saw taking place in the United States. Conservationists in both countries began to collaborate, which eventually led to treaties establishing certain species of marine mammals and migratory birds as international—rather than national—resources.

Because the approach was developed by the United States and Canada, that way of looking at wildlife is today known as the North American Model of Wildlife Conservation. The

Wildlife Society, a Bethesda, Maryland–based organization committed to wildlife stewardship through science and education, cites seven key tenets of the North American Model, among them that wildlife is an international public resource and should be protected by laws; that market hunting should be eliminated and wildlife killed only for legitimate purposes; that science should guide wildlife management policies; and that access to hunting should be available to everyone.

A position paper published in 2007 by the Wildlife Society notes that "unlike many other conservation models applied elsewhere in the world, hunting in the U.S. and Canada has remained open to all citizens regardless of class, and hunting has become central to the success of the model."

Along with the work of Audubon and others, that unusual conservation approach—one that embraced hunting as an important part of public wildlife policy—laid the groundwork to stop the wholesale killing that came in the early years of the twentieth century.

Between 1896 and 1898, concerned birders established Audubon Society chapters in Massachusetts, Pennsylvania, New York, New Hampshire, Illinois, Maine, Wisconsin, New Jersey, Rhode Island, Connecticut, Ohio, Indiana, Tennessee, Minnesota, Texas, and California, as well as in the District of Columbia.[13] Partly in reaction to the voracious Victorian-era appetite for bird-themed fashion, President Theodore Roosevelt in 1903 created the first national wildlife refuge, on Florida's Pelican Island. The National Audubon Society was incorporated in New York State two years later—the same year that Guy Bradley, one of the first Audubon wardens hired to protect Everglades roosting sites, was murdered by game poachers in Florida.[14] By the end of Teddy Roosevelt's second term, in 1909, he had created another fifty-one national wildlife refuges and firmly established the right, and responsibility, of the federal government to conserve wildlife and habitat, including wetlands for migratory waterfowl.[15] America was turning an important corner in its journey toward conservation awareness, but many battles lay ahead.

The federal government had passed the Lacey Act in 1900, making it a federal crime to poach game in one state with the purpose of selling the bounty in another—a direct attempt to discourage market hunting. The law also was concerned with the potential problems associated with introducing nonnative, or exotic, species of birds and animals into native ecosystems. Finally, it sought to support already existing state laws for the protection of game and birds. The Lacey Act had some teeth; violators faced stiff fines. Unfortunately, it presumed that states had strong wildlife-protection laws to begin with, when in fact many didn't. Lax enforcement by state authorities also was a problem.

Four years after the Lacey Act was passed, in 1904, a Pennsylvania congressman proposed a bill that advanced the notion that since birds migrated from state to state, only the federal government had the authority to manage and protect them. If this concept sounds vaguely familiar, it should. The idea is based on a long-controversial sixteen-word clause in the U.S. Constitution known as the "commerce clause,"[16] which has been endlessly debated, interpreted, and reinterpreted to help define the balance of power between the federal government and the states. Naturally, the so-called Bill to Protect Migratory Birds of the United States didn't sit well with states' rights proponents, who saw in it an insidiously encroaching federal authority.

But in some ways, the eventual failure of that bill and the tepid success of the earlier Lacey Act spurred conservation organizations to push for more federal initiatives. And where they had failed in the past to get their way, they eventually succeeded in 1913 by employing a time-honored tactic of American politics—deceit and subterfuge. After two congressmen introduced an even more comprehensive wildlife-protection proposal known as the Weeks-McLean bill, which seemed doomed to fail, its supporters attached it to a large agricultural appropriations bill that then sailed through both houses of a busy Congress, and Weeks-McLean was inadvertently signed into law by President William Taft, who had opposed it, in the waning hours of his presidency.

Wildlife supporters who'd finagled that bill into law with legislative trickery knew they were on thin ice. As stated in a section of the U.S. Fish and Wildlife Service website describing the history of migratory bird laws, "the Weeks-McLean Law rested on weak constitutional grounds."[17] So they set out to come up with a better legal rationale for protecting birds that didn't rely on a licentious interpretation of the Constitution's commerce clause.

The debate was still going on when, on October 21, 1916, the *New York Herald Tribune* published a cartoon by a then-unknown forty-year-old artist for the *Sioux City Journal* named Jay Norwood Darling, known to friends as Ding.[18] Titled "The Annual Migration of Duck Is On," it showed a solitary bird flying over a farm onto which had crowded perhaps a hundred hunters, who were firing their shotguns into the sky, turning it into what looked like a piece of overaged Swiss cheese.

It's impossible to say what impact that cartoon and Darling's other scathing pro-conservation drawings had on the national debate, but that same year the rock-solid legal strategy for which conservationists had been searching began to take shape.

The new legal strategy, delayed by the advent of World War I, was based on the U.S. president's clear right to enter into international treaties. Since 1913, the president had had the right to enter into treaties with other countries for the purpose of protecting migrating birds. Conservation supporters decided to put the bird-protection issue into a much broader context. They introduced the Migratory Bird Treaty Act, which simultaneously repealed Weeks-McLean and implemented the United States' commitment to a 1916 agreement with Canada for the protection of birds that migrated between Canada and the United States at some point during their annual life cycle. The act decreed that all migratory birds and their parts (including eggs, nests, and feathers) were fully protected. The act went into effect on July 3, 1918, and the Supreme Court upheld the validity of the law in 1920. For the Court, Justice Oliver Wendell Holmes Jr. wrote of the migrating birds, "The subject-matter is only transitorily within the state and has no permanent habitat therein. But for the treaty and the statute there soon might be no birds for any powers to deal with."[19]

You might think that the federal government, having cleared the last hurdle blocking its authority to manage migratory waterfowl, would have started making changes fast. But World

War I had drastically altered the American landscape—literally. The United States had responded to food shortages among its allies by draining critical wetlands for wheat production, and the U.S. population boomed in the prosperous years following the war's end in 1918. The nation already had drained a hundred million acres of wetlands during the first years of the twentieth century, and the postwar need for more housing, roads, and commercial development only made that problem worse.[20]

The decade that followed was a folly of land mismanagement. Farmers back then traditionally planted the same crops year after year, but that depleted soils of vital nutrients. Eventually the land became less productive, and fallow land is susceptible to erosion. In the wet American South, vast swaths became moonscapes of jagged, eroded gullies as topsoil washed away. Within a few years, the Great Plains were dealing with another, more dramatic problem, wind erosion, which eventually would shove America's waterfowl populations even closer to the brink, and also steal the spotlight from ongoing efforts to save them.

During the 1930s, a severe and prolonged drought took hold of much of the United States. Ponds in parts of the country where waterfowl populations flourished began to dry up, making those critical nesting and feeding habitats look less like paradise to migrating waterfowl and more like parched and barren desertscapes. In California, the drought extended from 1928 to 1937; in Missouri, from 1930 to 1941. Dust storms destroyed crops and farms, and the resulting agricultural depression helped accelerate the era's economic nightmares, including bank closures, business losses, and unemployment. It also created a great diaspora of families desperately searching for ways to survive.

America's heartland became a nation on the road, spurred by the same survival instinct that drives waterfowl to undertake their annual migrations.

Dust storms had been a problem for years in southeastern Colorado, southwestern Kansas, and the panhandles of Oklahoma and Texas. Fourteen such storms were recorded on the Great Plains in 1932, and thirty-eight storms the following year. By 1934, an estimated one hundred million acres of farmland had lost all or most of their topsoil to the winds, which whipped the dirt into what looked like mountain ranges on the move, huge "black blizzards" that scoured the fields, buried fences and tractors in drifts of once-fertile dirt, sent confused chickens to roost at midday, and scattered over hundreds of miles.

The wake-up call came on April 14, 1935. On that day, now known as Black Sunday, a storm with winds estimated at sixty miles an hour made the problem so big that even official Washington couldn't ignore it. In its aftermath came realities and cultural touchstones familiar even today, from the Woody Guthrie folk song "Dusty Old Dust" (which later became known as "So Long, It's Been Good to Know Yuh"), about the midwestern families who were forced to abandon their farms and migrate elsewhere, to John Steinbeck's 1939 masterpiece *The Grapes of Wrath*.

Black Sunday's wall of blowing sand and dust blasted into the eastern end of the Oklahoma panhandle in the far northwestern part of the state. Driven by winds of forty miles an hour or more, the roiling dust storm resembled what one account called "a land-based tsunami." In a *New Republic* article, reporter Avis D. Carlson wrote that such storms are "like a shovelful of fine sand flung against the face. People caught in their own yards grope for the doorstep. Cars come to a standstill, for no light in the world can penetrate that swirling murk . . . The nightmare is deepest during the storms. But on the occasional bright day and the usual gray day we cannot shake from it. We live with the dust, eat it, sleep with it, watch it strip us of possessions and the hope of possessions. It is becoming Real. The poetic uplift of spring fades into a phantom of the storied past. The nightmare is becoming life."[21] A report about the storm filed by an Associated Press reporter includes what is said to be one of the very first uses of a term that remains a part of the American lexicon: the Dust Bowl.

As absurd as it sounds, the memorable catchphrase and all that drama were just what the people pressing for soil conservation in America needed—and what proponents of migratory-waterfowl conservation measures sorely lacked. For example, in March 1935, several weeks before Black Sunday, one of President Franklin Roosevelt's advisers, Hugh Bennett, had testified before Congress about the need for better soil-conservation techniques. By the time Congress got around to voting on the Soil Conservation Act later that year, the massive Black Sunday storm had traveled all the way to the East Coast and was dimming the sun in the nation's capital. "Mr. Bennett only needed to point out the window to the evidence supporting his position, and say, 'This, gentlemen, is what I've been talking about,'" reads the National Weather Service account. "Congress passed the Soil Conservation Act before the end of the year."

For years, proponents of migratory-waterfowl conservation had been struggling along a parallel path toward protective federal legislation. Through the 1920s, the question of how to fund a series of wildlife refuges to better conserve and manage that natural resource had been kicked around Congress, with "kicked around" being the operative words. The grand idea of funding them with the sale of a federal hunting stamp was part of public discussion as early as 1920, when George Lawyer, the chief U.S. game warden, visited California. The state was the first to issue paper hunting licenses featuring hunting-themed designs,[22] and Lawyer recognized the program as a potential solution to the waterfowl-depletion problem. But attempts to put that idea into practice during the 1920s were routinely stomped to death by coalitions of states' rights defenders, private hunting clubs, and business interests, including gun and ammunition companies. In February 1929, Congress finally passed the Migratory Bird Conservation Act,[23] but it was a watered-down version of the original idea, and it had been stripped of many of the provisions that would have made it effective. Plus, it offered no clear way of generating funds to fulfill even its limited ambitions.

Besides, looming just around the corner was an American cataclysm that would eclipse everything else. The stock market crashed in October 1929, and the Great Depression soon was under way. By 1930, more pressing matters had pushed conservation efforts to the bottom of the public agenda. Between the collapsed economy and Dust Bowl devastation, the preoccupying issue for most Americans had become survival. Waterfowl protection? Sorry. Not a priority.

"This was a devastating time for migratory waterfowl," write Dolin and Dumaine in *The Duck Stamp Story.* "The resting, nesting, and feeding areas they relied on literally disappeared into thin air. Vast lakes were transformed into small ponds, and small ponds and swamplands turned into cracked mud. Where water did remain, other problems arose. As evaporation increased, high concentrations of alkaline salts made the water a deadly brew. Stagnant, fetid bodies of water, with masses of dying and decaying vegetation, provided a breeding ground for 'duck sickness,' or avian botulism. Waterfowl were dying in large numbers."[24]

Through it all, one voice never faded. During the late 1920s and into the 1930s, Ding Darling continued to pen scathing editorial cartoons that lamented the sorry plight of American waterfowl and stressed the need for effective conservation. In November 1932, with the election of Franklin Roosevelt to the American presidency, he got a powerful ally. Roosevelt, a Democrat, in 1933 appointed Darling to a special committee he'd created to study the waterfowl-conservation issue—a committee that also included scientist and scholar Aldo Leopold, who, along with David Brower, Rachel Carson, and a few others, today is regarded as one of the founders of American conservationism.

Darling's appointment made some question the new president's judgment. A cartoonist? Seriously? Equally confounding was that Darling was a stalwart Republican. When Roosevelt later offered Darling the job of head of the Bureau of Biological Survey (a forerunner of the U.S. Fish and Wildlife Service), some saw it as Roosevelt's cynical attempt to buy off someone often critical of his New Deal policies.

Darling didn't see it that way, and he set out to devise a program that would make hunters the primary stewards of the wildlife they hunted.

After fifteen years of fitful progress toward waterfowl conservation, things started happening as soon as Darling joined the administration. Eventual success came in two stages, the first beginning just six days after Darling took over in March 1934.[25] Something called the Migratory Bird Hunting and Conservation Stamp Act—a much-evolved version of earlier legislation—had made its way through Congress and landed on Roosevelt's desk. Commonly known as the Duck Stamp Act, the law would require each waterfowl hunter sixteen years of age or older to have a valid state hunting license and to buy a one-dollar federal hunting stamp to affix to their license or a special federal certificate, which, like the stamp itself, would be available at local post offices. The law also would require receipts from the sale of the stamp to be deposited in a special account known as the Migratory Bird Conservation Fund, with nearly every penny of that money to be used to lease or buy—and protect and maintain—habitat for migratory birds.

When Roosevelt signed the Duck Stamp Act on March 16, 1934, U.S. waterfowl populations were at or near an all-time low. But even the Duck Stamp Act was a classic Washington nonstarter; Darling knew that stamp revenue eventually would roll in, but he also knew how desperate the situation had become. He wanted to get critical wetlands under federal control before even more of them were lost to farming or development, but he had a hard time making good on Roosevelt's vague promise to provide one million dollars for the acquisition of some critical wetlands. He spent months getting the runaround from various administration officials while trying to convert Roosevelt's IOU into cash. But while Darling was new as a Washington insider, he was no political naïf. He eventually resorted to the kind of political subterfuge of which D.C. legends are made.

The second stage of his success in establishing the Duck Stamp Program took place on a single day in early June 1935. The full story is complicated, involving both a last-minute alliance with a sympathetic Senator Peter Norbeck, a South Dakota Democrat, and Norbeck's surreptitious insertion of Darling's funding request into a much broader bill for the Bureau of Biological Survey. And since they were back-channeling the whole thing anyway, Norbeck—what the heck?—bumped the request from the one million dollars Roosevelt had promised to six million. He then artfully steered the bill through a brief airing on the Senate floor. By that afternoon, the wily, duck-loving senator had steered it just as artfully past the Appropriations Committee and onto the desk of Roosevelt, who was scheduled to leave the next day for a Caribbean fishing trip.

Maybe Roosevelt truly grasped the importance of the funding request and decided to make waterfowl protection a priority in the midst of the Great Depression. Or maybe, as most accounts suggest, Roosevelt simply signed the bill without reading it carefully, then headed off on vacation.

Either way, the deed was done. The federal government had previously established its legal authority to manage the nation's wildlife; it had enacted a law specifically designed to protect migratory waterfowl; and it had come up with a way to fund that mission that was as simple as it was brilliant and that made America's hunters primarily responsible for the cost of conserving the nation's wildlife resources.

According to Darling's good-humored accounting in a July 26, 1935, letter to Roosevelt—complete with a caricature of the president and other cartoon figures—the six million dollars was going to be used to buy the 400,000-acre Okefenokee Swamp in southern Georgia and northern Florida (now the Okefenokee National Wildlife Refuge), one of the oldest and best-preserved freshwater systems in America. Its cypress forests, marshes, lakes, and islands are filled with alligators, sandhill cranes, red-cockaded woodpeckers, and more than four hundred other species of animals. The money also was used to buy private land to create the 278,000-acre Hart Mountain National Antelope Refuge, northeast of Lakeview, Oregon, which is home to more than three hundred species of wildlife, including pronghorn antelope, California bighorn sheep, mule deer, sage grouse, and redband trout; to expand the winter elk range in Jackson Hole, Wyoming; and to repair the dams and dikes in various duck ranges already under Darling's bureau's management.

Three days later, Roosevelt penned an equally good-humored note to Darling on White House stationery that began, "As I was saying to the Acting Director of the Budget the other day—'this fellow Darling is the only man in history who got an appropriation through Congress, past the Budget and signed by the President without anybody realizing that the Treasury had been raided.' You hold an all-time record."

That was the beginning. With additional legislative steps forward, including the 1958 creation of the Small Wetlands Acquisition Program specifically to conserve small, unconnected parcels known as waterfowl production areas (located mostly within the north-central region of the country), the United States came to have an innovative conservation program that would eventually become the envy of the world. Today, the annual revenue that drives the program comes from three sources: the sale of Federal Duck Stamps to hunters, collectors, and conservation supporters; import duties on arms and ammunition; and a percentage of refuge entrance fees.

All these years later, nearly half of that money comes from the sale of duck stamps. It's deposited in the Migratory Bird Conservation Fund, and a realty division within the National Wildlife Refuge System is charged with identifying important wetlands and other habitat areas. The federal Migratory Bird Conservation Commission prioritizes and authorizes those areas for purchase or lease. Since 1934, the Fish and Wildlife Service has spent more than a billion dollars from the Migratory Bird Conservation Fund to permanently protect 5.3 million acres of critical waterfowl habitat—including more than twenty-six thousand waterfowl production areas, averaging 223 acres in size, located mostly in the Dakotas, Montana, Minnesota, Michigan, Nebraska, Iowa, and Wisconsin. In 2009 alone, the service used nearly fifty-one million dollars from the fund to add more than 12,000 acres of waterfowl habitat at migratory bird refuges and almost 30,000 acres in what's officially known as the Prairie Pothole Region, bringing the total number of conserved acres in that favorite waterfowl migration area to nearly 700,000.

Wildlife experts and conservationists still marvel at the simple audacity of the idea. "You've got to remember the Duck Stamp was created in 1934, at a time when people were hiding their money in mattresses," says Ducks Unlimited's Dale Hall, adding that the protections extended to waterfowl later were expanded to fish and other wildlife. "People had killed off almost all the wildlife in the depression to feed their families. There's no judgment from me on that one. If you're trying to keep your child fed, you're going to go out and shoot the deer and the turkey and the game that's out there."

That context makes the formation of the Duck Stamp Program all the more remarkable, Hall says, recalling that the first edition of the stamp cost a dollar. "A dollar back then would probably get the staples for a family of five or six for a week or longer." And yet, hunters—and eventually the gun and ammunition makers—"stood together and said, 'First and foremost, we're conservationists, and we know somebody's gotta pay' . . . They said, 'You can make us pay a dollar to go hunting as long as that money goes to buy habitat.'"

Unfortunately, with the declining number of hunters and the rising cost of land, the program's ability to protect habitat is diminished. The cost of a duck stamp has held steady at fifteen dollars since 1991. Since 1998, though, the price of land in the Prairie Pothole Region, for example, has more than tripled. To stop the erosion of duck stamp buying power, Congressmen John Dingell and Robert Wittman introduced H.R. 1916, the Migratory Bird Habitat Investment and Enhancement Act, in April 2009. It would have amended the Migratory Bird Hunting and Conservation Stamp Act to increase the stamp price to twenty-five dollars between 2010 and 2020, then to thirty-five dollars thereafter. But the bill fell to the bottom of the priority list for the 111th Congress, and with annual duck stamp sales projected to drop by two million dollars in 2011,[26] Fish and Wildlife began scrambling to get a price increase through legislative means.

Still, the Duck Stamp Program chugs along, "the little program that could," in program chief Pat Fisher's words, adding acre by acre, year by year, to the extraordinary National Wildlife Refuge System.

Along the way, though, someone came up with the equally

brilliant idea of having an annual art contest to determine the design of each year's Federal Duck Stamp. And seventeen years after opening the contest to everyone, organizers decided in 1966 to open the judging process to the public as well.

And that's when things got infinitely more interesting.

*4*

# ROUND ONE

A T PRECISELY TEN A.M., with the 180-seat auditorium
of Berkeley's David Brower Center only about half full,
Paul Schmidt, assistant director of the U.S. Fish and Wildlife
Service's Migratory Bird Program, steps to the podium. For the
occasion, it has been rigged with the service's official seal and
decorated with an arrangement of dried grasses. Several last-
minute wrinkles have by now been ironed out, including a Fish
and Wildlife staffer's scramble to locate the Stars and Stripes for
the presentation of the colors and the playing of the national
anthem.

"You're in the worst possible place to try to find an American flag," someone had told her, so the AV guy downloaded a
video clip of a waving flag and a stirring version of the anthem
(complete with the roar of a sports stadium crowd during the
final notes) just minutes before the program began. Now, at
last, it's time for the first of three scheduled rounds of judging
for the 2010 Federal Duck Stamp Contest—save for some welcoming remarks by Schmidt and other dignitaries, including
the service's Pacific Southwest regional director, the mayor of
Berkeley, and the Brower Center's executive director, as well as

Schmidt's introduction of the contest judges and an official explanation of the judging procedures by Larry Mellinger, an attorney from the Interior Department's Office of the Solicitor.

"This is a milestone year for the Federal Duck Stamp Contest," says Schmidt, the master of ceremonies for an opening round that's equal parts high mass, casting call, and slaughterhouse. "Other than one time, when we were barely west of the Mississippi River, this is the first time we've *really* been west of the Mississippi and on the West Coast, and we're happy to be here in California, where we know that not just art but waterfowl are a big part of the culture and climate."

The printed contest program includes a welcome from Rowan Gould, acting director of the Fish and Wildlife Service, who emphasizes why California's San Francisco Bay Area is "a unique backdrop" for the competition. Neither Schmidt's nor Gould's words, though, hint at the more practical reason the 2010 finals are being staged in Berkeley: the increasingly critical need to educate people other than hunters about the program, to convince the unlikely constituencies of birders and other "nonconsumptive" conservationists to join hunters in supporting a program that for nearly eight decades has effectively and admirably served the goals of both groups. Schmidt reminds the crowd that the duck stamp represents "one of the most significant and successful conservation programs ever created" and that it has created an unparalleled conservation legacy.

"Whether you're a waterfowl hunter, birder, hiker, collector, or just someone who enjoys art, this is a way for you to contribute through the purchase of those duck stamps in a simple and lasting way, and continue the legacy of David Brower, Rachel Carson, Ding Darling, and so many other conservationists."

Schmidt gestures to his left, to a somber row of five judging stations. The long table has been draped in a stately blue cover also featuring the service's official seal. Each judging station is partitioned from the others by a black panel, so that the audience can see all five judges but the judges cannot see one another's work space. Each station includes a gooseneck desk lamp to illuminate the original paintings as they're presented to each judge; a reducing glass to help the judge imagine how a painting might look when shrunk to the size of a one-and-three-quarter-inch-long, one-and-a-half-inch-wide duck stamp; and a small video monitor upon which will display scanned versions of each of the 235 paintings, in case a judge wants to consider any of them for longer than the brief seconds during which the original painting will be presented. Each station also has two placards that hint at the brutal cull about to take place.

One reads, "In."

The other reads, "Out."

Schmidt introduces Ren Lohoefener, the director of the Fish and Wildlife Service's Pacific Southwest region, who steps to the podium.

"There are many ways to measure the worth of the Duck Stamp Contest and the worth of the duck stamp, and one of the ways is in what they do," he says. "You know, ninety-eight percent of the funds raised go to work in conservation of habitat for wildlife. And that's a pretty amazing percentage. I don't know of any other [program] in any government that can say they put ninety-eight percent of the funds they raise actually out there on the ground. Two percent for an administrative overhead is just incredibly small. So that's one way to measure duck stamps."

Lohoefener notes the millions of acres of habitat that have

been conserved using duck stamp funds, including more than four hundred thousand in California, where sixteen national wildlife refuges have benefited. "That is a *lot* of area," he says. "More than eight million—eight million!—duck stamps have been purchased since 1934 by Californians. That surprised me. That's second only to Minnesota. So those are things we can measure and talk about."

Even more critical, he says, is the program's ability to communicate the beauty of wildlife and the need for conservation through art, an "amazing way to reach out." He lauds the Junior Duck Stamp Contest for conveying that message to America's younger generations, and the thirty-four states that have replicated the conservation-stamp idea and now produce state wildlife stamps that prove a hunter has paid the necessary state licensing fee. "Stamps that promote native trout. Stamps that promote their threatened and endangered species. One of the stamps you'll see out there on sale today, and I hope you'll take a look at it, is [a fund-raiser] for the Gulf of Mexico and the recent oil spill down there."

When the 2010 contest year began at the conclusion of the 2009 contest, no one could have predicted the messy, depressing, and deadly drama that would soon be unfolding in the critical wetlands rimming the gulf. But the BP spill in April had gushed oil for almost three months, and by the time the spill had been temporarily capped in July, Louisiana's Breton National Wildlife Refuge was awash in sludge. Other refuges and national parks were threatened, birds were dying, and the resources of the Fish and Wildlife Service were being stretched thin while those who understood the stakes tried to mitigate the disaster. In his welcoming statement in the contest program, acting director Gould has singled out this environmental disaster that is casting a long shadow over the nation's conservation efforts in 2010.

At this point in a pep talk by a bureaucrat, you might expect the auditorium to be buzzing with the idle chatter of those who've lost interest. But the assembled audience sits in rapt, stone silence, listening. Lohoefener then recalls a brand of cereal he ate as a kid. There, before the crowd in Berkeley, the name of the cereal escapes him. But, he says, "Inside the box of cereal were these little cards, about the size of baseball cards." They were prints of paintings featuring birds. "They were alive in your hand, and I'll never ever forget the impact that that had on me. The impact those artists have had on conservation through their beautiful paintings is phenomenal."

In closing, Lohoefener acknowledges the sixteen California artists who are participating in this year's contest, as well as the two previous federal winners from the state, Robert Steiner and Sherrie Russell Meline, seemingly unaware that both are seated just steps from him in the dim auditorium.

The strong presence of California artists this year masks one of the more startling realities of the contest: Even though the state is the most populous in the nation, with about thirty-eight million residents in 2010, its participation in the Federal Duck Stamp Contest pales when compared with that of relatively tiny Minnesota, the unquestioned center of the duck stamp universe, where the 2010 population is estimated to be slightly more than five million. More than 12 percent of this year's Duck Stamp Contest entries have come from Minnesota, the heart of North America's most prolific waterfowl-producing region. California has come in second, with just over 7 percent of the entries, followed by Florida and Ohio (5 percent each), Wisconsin (4.7 percent), Pennsylvania and New York (4.2 percent), Missouri (3.8 percent), and Michigan and Texas (3.4 percent). Minnesota's statistical dominance also carries over into the purchase figures for Federal Duck Stamps. Between 1934 and 2003, for example, the more than nine million stamps sold in Minnesota dwarfed the numbers sold in much more populous states, including California (8.2 million) and Texas (7.6 million).

Minnesota's central role in the Duck Stamp Program and the subculture it has spawned owes its origins to geographic realities that make the state the capital of North American duck country.

Most species of waterfowl tend to be more comfortable either dabbling along the surface of a pond, marsh, or river or diving down beneath it than they are in the air. While some species are strong, swift, and graceful on the wing, many flap manically across the sky during migration, desperately airborne. They're like preschoolers on a long road trip—constantly looking for places to stop, eat, and rest. Many waterfowl fight a doomed battle to stay aloft, afflicted by what professional pilots describe as an unfortunate "wing load ratio."

"It's just the way a duck is built," explains John Solberg, the now-retired Fish and Wildlife Service pilot and biologist. "From a pilot's perspective, there's a term called 'wing loading,' which is the ratio of the weight of the airplane to the surface area of the wing. A heavier airplane with a relatively smaller wing is going to require more power to stay flying."

Many ducks and geese are cargo-loaded Boeing C-17 Globemaster IIIs borne aloft on stubby Cessna wings. They're heavy compared to most birds and have small wings, so their engines need to be large and powerful to compensate. "That's why ducks have plump, pronounced breasts compared to some of the song-birds," Solberg says. "It takes a lot of muscle to sustain flight. They have to flap a lot to stay in the air."

The wing load problem is particularly pronounced in diving ducks, such as scaup, redheads, and canvasbacks, which typically are graceless flyers.

"It's very evident when they take off," Solberg says. "A dabbling duck springs off the water, straight into the air. A diving duck runs across the water's surface while flapping its wings to reach the flight speed needed to overcome gravity."

Waterfowl have discovered ways, once airborne, to make migration more energy efficient and safer. They understand that there's safety in numbers, and while they don't flock en masse as some geese do—ducks generally travel in small flocks of five to twenty birds—they're still able to take advantage of multiple eyes scanning for predators and the collected wisdom of experienced individuals. Plus, Solberg says, by flying in those familiar V formations, ducks are displaying their awareness of the science of energetics.

"Just based on aerodynamics, there's thought to be some benefit in some of the formations they fly in," he says. "The bird behind gets beneficial lift from the bird preceding him, kind of like a race car driver drafting off the car in front of him. The guy in front breaks up the wind, so the guy in back doesn't have to work as hard to move the same distance."

But gravity is only part of their problem. Driven by the biological imperatives to eat and breed, ducks and other waterfowl are constantly on the move. And they're not shy about claiming vast swaths of North America as their territory. Their migration to their northern breeding grounds begins in late March or early April. As the snow and ice in the colder climates begin to melt, the flocks move from the southern United States and Mexico up into the north-central parts of the United States and Canada, where in wet years the snowmelt and rain fill what are known as prairie potholes—a seemingly endless patchwork of depressions in the landscape left behind about ten thousand years ago by receding glaciers. The Prairie Pothole Region is so important in terms of wetland conservation that it's known unofficially, at least in waterfowl-management circles, as the "duck factory" of North America.[1]

Minnesota is the factory's production floor. Fly northwest out of Minneapolis International Airport, for example, and before long you have a bird's-eye view of duck paradise. Shallow little ponds dimple the landscape, in some cases seventy or eighty per square mile,[2] each one an inviting freshwater rest stop and smorgasbord of duck food for tired, hungry birds. When the sun shines, the ponds can glimmer like water beading on the hood of a car. During wet years, it's easy to imagine the landscape as a vast sea studded with islands rather than a pond-pocked prairie.

What you see from your airplane window once was the greatest expanse of grasslands and small wetlands on the planet. It still covers sixty-four million acres; you can fly from north-central Iowa; through Minnesota, the Dakotas, and Montana; and across the Canadian provinces of Manitoba, Saskatchewan, and Alberta and never leave the Prairie Pothole Region. And even today, with significant portions of the original wetlands and grasslands converted to agriculture and many potholes drained or filled with dirt to create plowable, plantable fields, the region still provides breeding grounds for more than 60 percent of the key migratory bird species in the United States. According to a recent report by the federal Government Accountability Office, it also provides critical habitat for nearly two hundred migratory bird species, including some, such as the piping plover and the whooping crane, that are threatened or endangered.[3]

The words "habitat" and "ecosystem" have been so overused by the world's armchair eco-warriors that they've nearly lost their meaning. But according to Solberg, the Prairie Pothole Region is a perfect case study of how important the webs of interlocking natural realities can be. During drought years in the region, the sun dries up the ponds, and plant and other organic material in them is broken down and reabsorbed into the earth. The grasslands dry out as well, and occasional fires help release nutrients back into the soil, making it even more rich and fertile.

When a harsh winter follows, the frozen earth creates a concretelike frost seal beneath the potholes. After a heavy snowfall, the dry potholes are recharged with runoff, and the stage is set for a waterfowl bacchanal. "The potholes are most productive after they've been dry for a year or two," Solberg says. That triggers what he describes as an "explosion of invertebrates" such as flies, midges, and freshwater shrimp. In duck-food terms, invertebrates are the equivalent of filet mignon, little energy bombs that Solberg says provide three to four times as much protein as plants. To an overflying duck, full prairie potholes are like bright, glowing interstate exit signs advertising a free all-you-can-eat buffet.

The combination of abundant water, nesting cover, and

available food is a perfect and precise formula for ducks and other waterfowl seeking to breed and hatch their eggs each year. "When there's water on the prairie landscape, especially combined with large patches of grass, it provides huge numbers of available nesting locations," Solberg says. "It's incredible."

This is precisely the cycle Solberg says began during back-to-back wet winters in 2008–2009 and 2009–2010. By the spring of 2010, as the 235 artists began pondering their entries for the 2010 Federal Duck Stamp Contest, large portions of the duck factory were in full and glorious production. The marshy areas provided perfect cover for nesting—many ducks like their space and privacy in such matters—and the hens were busy ingesting huge amounts of protein during the process of laying eggs and raising ducklings. The ducklings, too, were busy gobbling those high-protein invertebrates because, as mid-level members of a food chain that included foxes, raccoon, mink, and other predators, their survival depended on growing quickly, learning to fly, and preparing to migrate to warmer climates when winter rolled around again.

But what should have been an affirmation that decades of conservation efforts with duck stamp money were having their desired effect was muted by the Gulf of Mexico oil-spill disaster. The good news, according to Solberg: Ducks aren't particularly ambitious, and therefore fewer of them were likely to migrate all the way to the gulf in the fall of 2010. Unlike geese and some other waterfowl, which are programmed to migrate vast distances to familiar locations based on mysterious biological and celestial clocks, ducks are basically looking for a good time. When the weather gets too cold in the winter, they'll move south until they can find unfrozen ponds and available food. "If there's open water on the rivers and small grains are available in the farm fields, they'll hang around and put up with temperatures well below freezing as long as their food source isn't covered by snow," Solberg says. "They move only as far as they need to to find water to roost and food to survive. They may only have to move a hundred miles, and they'll stay at the spot for a week or two." He adds, "Survival remains their first order of business throughout their lives."

Anxious artists from around the country, including those gathered in Berkeley and others following the Duck Stamp Contest webcast on their home computers, await the start of the first round of judging. Emcee Paul Schmidt takes a moment at the Brower Center podium to acknowledge the presence of twenty-year duck stamp collector Murray Touche, who since 1998 has missed the contest judging only twice—a feat that might not be all that remarkable except that Touche travels all the way from his home in Scotland for the event. "We keep moving this further and further away from him, and he still comes and enjoys it every year. So, Murray, thanks for coming yet again."

Then it's time to introduce the judges, whose names until this morning have not been publicly revealed, by both tradition and official dictate from program chief Pat Fisher, who wants to make sure no competing artists or collectors try to contact or manipulate the judges. ("Sorry, I cannot divulge names," Fisher said three weeks before the finals. "If you want to get me fired, this would be a really quick way to accomplish it.") Schmidt explains that the five judges will, during the next two days, have the unenviable task of winnowing the 235 submitted pieces down to a single winner. "We'll be watching here, but also we'll be streaming this for the first time, so people across the country—not to put any pressure on you—will be watching your selection."

Schmidt summons Mike Chrisman from the wings. The tall and graying director of the Southwestern Partnership Offices for the National Fish and Wildlife Foundation strides confidently toward the partitioned judging table. He oversees the foundation's habitat programs in California, Nevada, Utah, Colorado, New Mexico, and Arizona. A fourth-generation Californian and a partner in his family's ranching and farming business, he also served as the state's secretary of natural resources, advising then-governor Arnold Schwarzenegger on issues related to California's natural, historic, and cultural resources. Chrisman takes his place at the judging station nearest the podium, the first introduced member of a judging panel that, as Jim Hautman suspected it would, looks like it may have a Western flavor.

Next called is John Eadie. His professorship in waterfowl biology at the University of California, Davis, is named after Dennis G. Raveling, an internationally recognized waterfowl academic and researcher who died in 1991. Eadie specializes in, among other things, avian ecology, waterfowl management and conservation, population ecology, animal behavior, conservation genetics, and wetland ecology. But he's no mere academician; he's working hard to bridge the gap between the people who talk the talk about waterfowl habitat conservation and the people who since 1934 have been walking the walk by paying for it.

For example, Eadie helped create an innovative "student hunter camp" program with the California Waterfowl Association that in January 2010 enrobed UC Davis wildlife majors in camouflage hunting gear, thrust shotguns into their hands, and sent them off for a weekend of firearms education and duck hunting in Northern California's woods and marshes. The program was a way to teach the conservation-minded students about the vital role that hunters play in conservation, and also to acquaint the students with the hunting culture that could be a critical part of their professional lives. (Wrote student Amanda Culpepper afterward, "In a short period of time, I metamorphosed from someone who believed hunters were pretty scary, to a person who believes hunters are amazing and admirable people. It really was a transformative event for me, and I would do it again in a heartbeat.")

Eadie is followed to the judging table by Joe Garcia. Balding and bearded, the gregarious Garcia's white ponytail gives him a scruffy, boho look that sets him apart from the other judges, despite his conservative dark blazer and khaki pants. The landscape and wildlife artist from Julian, in California's San Diego County, worked as a commercial illustrator for thirteen years before choosing to focus full-time on painting as a career, and his presence is clearly intended to bring an artist's perspective to the panel's later between-round discussions.

When introduced, Jerry Serie steps from the wings and takes his place at the center spot of the judging table. The Minnesota native, a passionate hunter and fisherman since he was a kid, retired from the Fish and Wildlife Service in 2007 after thirty-five years as a wildlife biologist working on migratory bird conservation. Now living in Easton, Maryland, he actively promoted the North American Waterfowl Management Plan during his career and worked with Canadian federal and provincial agencies to promote the international coordination of migratory bird initiatives. Serie's unsmiling entrance conveys the same stolid, no-nonsense presence you get with Chicago Bears legend Mike Ditka.

The final judge introduced is Carlo Vecchiarelli, a somewhat dour-looking man who retired in 2003 as dean of the Math, Computer Science and Engineering Division of the Chabot–Las Positas Community College District, in Pleasanton, California. The wildlife biologist and lifelong member of the California Waterfowl Association has been involved in the sale and distribution of duck stamps and prints for more than thirty years, and he wrote and published *U.S. Duck Stamps*, one of the first books about Federal Duck Stamps. He takes his seat immediately to Serie's right, and the two of them lend a certain Soviet-era gravity to the panel.

With all five judges now at their posts, and alternate judge Gary Kramer, a retired manager of the Sacramento National Wildlife Refuge Complex, seated in the audience, having pronounced himself "ready to go if somebody goes down," the Western flavor of the panel is apparent. Four of the five judges, and the only alternate, are Californians.

Looking on, Pat Fisher quietly pronounces the five men arrayed at the front of the auditorium "one of our most qualified judging panels ever." The Western skew, she says, is not the result of some grand design. Rather, she says, using judges who live in the region where the event will be held cuts down on costs. Regardless of the reason, Jim Hautman guessed correctly about the type of people who would be judging his painting.

Schmidt offers a few final, cautionary words to the audience.

"The judges, you'll note, are screened from one another. We're encouraging them not to consult one another or talk amongst themselves. They're to use their skills, their observations, their judgment, in selecting what they think is the piece of art that should grace the Federal Duck Stamp for the next year. We don't want them to influence one another, and we don't want you to influence them. So—and I know it's kind of unusual in a competition of this sort; maybe it's more like tennis than football— we're asking you to be kind of quiet and just observe. If you would, please keep from oohing and aahing or booing or throwing anything or cheering. They've got a tough job to do, so let's let them work as a panel to do that."

One final bureaucrat, Larry Mellinger, from the solicitor's office at Interior, steps to the podium. The proceedings take on an official tone as he reviews the judging procedure.

In Round One, Mellinger says, he and an assistant will take turns passing each of the entries in front of the judges, in the order they were received through the mail at the Federal Duck Stamp Program office. The first painting entered will be judged first; the second, second; and so on. At the same time, the entry being judged will be projected onto the large screen suspended above and behind the five judges.

After each judge has had the opportunity to view the painting itself and a projection of it on the small monitor in front of them, they will be asked to vote, Mellinger says. Their choices are limited to an unforgiving two: They must vote the painting either "In" or "Out." Three or more "In" votes, and the piece will move on to the second round. Less than that, and the artist's dream for 2010 is likely to die then and there. Unless . . .

"There is kind of a Part B of Round One," Mellinger explains.

The contest rules stipulate that, following the first round, each judge may bring back up to five entries that, for whatever reason, did not make it through the first round of voting. Those who've watched the contests over the years say the voting process sometimes creates inexplicable anomalies in which strong and potentially competitive paintings are cast into the heap of first-round casualties. The second-chance rule allows each judge to bring back overlooked-but-worthy entries that somehow failed to generate the three "In" votes needed to advance to the second round. The rule is intended to at least partially offset judge fatigue from making hundreds of evaluations in such a short amount of time. Any eliminated paintings that get such a reprieve will be announced before the competition resumes the next morning.

Mellinger also previews the rules for Round Two of the judging, then pauses ever so slightly. The preliminaries are over. His assistant, Marie Strassburger, picks up a painting, the first to have arrived at the program headquarters in Arlington. Created by an artist named Katie Helms, of Monroe, North Carolina, it must feel surprisingly light for something so freighted with aspiration. "If the judges are ready to begin work," Mellinger says, "we will begin the 2010 Federal Duck Stamp Contest with Entry Number One."

What happens next has all the rigid formality of a Japanese tea ceremony. At ten forty-five A.M., a reverential hush falls over the audience in the dim auditorium as Strassburger hands Mellinger the Helms painting. It shows a bird standing in what looks like snow.

With his back to the audience, Mellinger moves down the line of five judges, presenting the artwork to each in turn as if it were some sort of sacred relic—an admirable courtesy that will be extended to every one of the entries, no matter how well or poorly executed. The painting also is projected larger than life onto the giant video screen behind the panel. Less than thirty-nine seconds later, with each judge having assessed the Helms piece for ten seconds or less—not counting any time the judges spent previewing the painting online or in the temporary gallery outside the Brower Center auditorium—Mellinger stands to the side and presents Helms's painting to the audience. He then issues a single command:

"Please vote."

Each judge reaches for one of the two first-round placards. Raised high above the panel's heads, five white "Out" placards glow against a black background. The results are shown on the giant screen.

"It's out," Mellinger announces solemnly as Strassburger steps forward at the other end of the judging table with Entry No. 2. She presents artist Anthony Morgan's depiction of two ruddy ducks on a pond to the first judge, and the process begins again. The bloodletting continues as Morgan's entry and the next—Richland, New Jersey, artist Joanna Rivera's pair of flying shovelers over a sunlit lake—are voted "Out."

Entry No. 4 is a rhinestone-studded, hologram-billed shoveler assembled almost entirely from corporate and other logos that the painter, avant-garde Minneapolis artist Rob McBroom, found visually interesting. The audience greets its appearance on the big screen with the same reverent silence that it offered the previous three, but the piece is clearly so off-key in this lineup of painstakingly realistic paintings of waterfowl that it might as well be a painting of a Pontiac Firebird. Seeing it makes Pat Fisher smile; she's familiar with McBroom's annual effort and says she looks forward to it. But the judges don't spend a lot of time pondering his glittering and sardonic attempt to bridge the gap between the worlds of avant-garde and wildlife art. The painting moves down the row of judges in a swift and decisive twenty-three seconds before the "Please vote" command is issued.

The five resounding "Out" votes are not entirely unexpected by anyone, especially McBroom, who, during a decade of competing for the Duck Stamp Artist title, has earned only one "In" vote. That came from a judge several contests ago who the artist says had an oh-what-the-hell sense of humor.

"It's out."

The logjam breaks, finally, with Entry No. 5, a pair of ruddy ducks on a placid pond by Adam Oswald, a self-described "wild-life and golf artist" from Pierre, South Dakota. The judges give it three "In" votes, and it moves to the second round. But it's a rare exception.

First-round judging continues for the rest of the morning and—after a fifty-minute lunch break—into the afternoon as the judges consider each of the year's entries. Sporadic murmurs accompany the announcements of the most stunning paintings, and the audience occasionally gasps as unknowns are elevated and favorites are eliminated. Despite a constant low tension in the room, there's no denying the fatigue factor that some artists consider when deciding how to position their entry in a contest in which the paintings are judged in the order of their arrival. About halfway through the afternoon judging, the unmistakable sound of one audience member's snoring triggers a few nudges and smiles. And judges, too, are susceptible to fatigue. While voting on Entry No. 194, for example, judge Carlo Vecchiarelli inadvertently raises his "Out" placard upside down.

The first-round judging in the 2010 contest, it turns out, is the metaphorical equivalent of market hunting. The judges wield their "Out" placards without mercy, like those lead-shot-spewing punt guns that nineteenth-century profiteers used to decimate entire flocks of waterfowl. Fatal "Out" votes come with startling swiftness and finality. Only twenty-eight paintings survive the first-round carnage, and more than half of the 235 competitors suffer the ignominy of receiving five "Out" votes.

It's impossible to say what factors each judge considers in ruling out specific paintings, but a few discernible preferences and prejudices are worth noting:

- Photo-realism clearly remains the style of choice. For example, Entry No. 51, an elegant and minimalist depiction of a Canada goose by Fort Bragg, North Carolina, artist Kristie Madsen, has no discernible background. It receives five "Out" votes in the first round. Same with Entry No. 209, a floating-Canada-goose painting dominated by a fire-engine-red dragonfly in the foreground. It looks like a scene the Disney Studios might have animated.
- Risk takers typically are not rewarded. Entry No. 91, for example, depicts a pair of Canada geese flying against a dawn space shuttle liftoff. It is unceremoniously goose-

egged with five "Out" votes. Entry No. 87, showing two ruddy ducks floating amid tendrils of vapor rising off a pond, has an unfortunate duck soup quality and gets five "Out" votes as well.

• Less is more, especially in a painting that will need to translate visually when reduced to stamp size. Only one painting featuring more than two ducks survives the first round, and that's a close-up of a single Canada goose by former winner Sherrie Russell Meline. She has included two other geese in flight in the distance, but they're just part of the background rather than characters in the scene. Generally, paintings with multiple birds do not fare well, including one showing an entire squadron of specklebelly geese that looks like it's waiting for air-traffic-control clearance to land at O'Hare. Another painting of five Canada geese standing in a cornfield in what looks like marching formation triggers five "Out" votes.

• Homages don't often work, even if well executed. Intentionally or not, the artist behind Entry No. 66 has turned in a piece that brings to mind the 1959–1960 King Buck stamp, featuring Maynard Reece's painting of a champion black Lab holding a limp duck in its mouth. No. 66, which shows an alert black Lab gazing over the back of what appears to be a decoy Canada goose at a real goose in flight, receives only a single "In" vote. One of the most memorable duck stamps features Adam Grimm's 1999 painting of a sun-kissed mottled duck rising up off the water and spreading its wings. The pose was unlike any that had come before it, and it was so unforgettable that it should probably be retired from competition. Three 2010 competitors have attempted a similar pose. Combined, they receive a total of only one "In" vote.

On the other hand, some paintings soar through the first round, including six that manage four out of five "In" votes each and four paintings that receive all five "In" votes. One of these exceptional four is Washington State artist Dee Dee Murry's painting of a solitary, sunlit Canada goose standing against a backdrop of gray storm clouds, a pose and lighting dynamic that have some of the same qualities as Jim Hautman's painting of specklebellies. Another of the four is a painting of two swimming shovelers submitted by 1984 contest winner Gerald Mobley of Oklahoma, always a formidable competitor.

Two other paintings receive five first-round "In" votes. While few in the room know it at the time, including the five judges, there seems a certain inevitability to the fact that both are Hautmans.

# THE SECOND BATTLE OF
# SPECKLEBELLY

IN APRIL 2010, about four months before the contest dead-line, Bob Hautman is sitting in a converted henhouse on his 120-acre Delano, Minnesota, farm, talking about various things on his mind. Many of his competitors have been working on their entries for months, but despite the approaching deadline and the pressure to help uphold the family rep, little on Hautman's mind this early spring day has anything to do with duck stamps.

First, he has fifteen dead birds in his Sears Kenmore freezer. Not that that's unusual, but it *is* becoming a problem. "Wife doesn't like it much," he says.

Some of them he shot himself; others were gifts. A few blundered into his studio's sliding glass door. He mentions more than once that keeping those accident-prone unfortunates to use as models for his work is against the law. But his main concern at the moment is the pheasant he's been using for a painting in progress.

"I thawed it out, then made this contraption to spread the wings out. Then I refroze it that way. It's huge, takes up about half the top of the freezer. I gotta get it out of there. She really doesn't like it. Every time she opens it up to get something, there's this big ol' rooster in there.''

The dead, spread-eagled marriage stressor in his Kenmore isn't the only thing preoccupying Bob Hautman on this gray spring day. Taller and rangier than brother Jim, and with a slightly receding hairline, he's wearing old jeans and a long-sleeve cotton shirt. He looks and sounds vaguely like actor Luke Wilson, and has the same laconic wit and athletic build. And at fifty one, he's training for his first half marathon, running five days a week.

"I made a bet with Jim," he says.

The brothers had been at a party about five weeks before. Someone there had mentioned his plan to run in a half marathon. To someone as competitive as Bob, it was a challenge too hard to resist. He said he'd run it too. "And Jim said, 'You couldn't do that.' So I made a bet with him. Now we're only ten days out, and I've gotta be able to do thirteen miles."

Then there's the pond problem. He has several scattered among the farm's wooded acres, but he'd got this idea to dig one right outside his studio, to lure birds close enough to watch and photograph. Somehow, he'd got it wrong. At the moment, the pond is choked with cattails. "Didn't quite work out like I wanted." The pasture next to his studio into which he sometimes drives golf balls is looking a little undermaintained as well.

His 2010 Duck Stamp Contest painting? Oh, that. Way down on the priority list. "I mean, I can tell you right now, I'm thinking about geese. But I really don't know what I'm gonna do."

Months pass. In early July, just four weeks before the deadline, Hautman claims he's still dithering. "I think I'm gonna do the specklebelly. It's a striking bird, and I've never painted one.

I've toyed around with the shoveler, but nothing has worked out yet. If I don't work something out in the next couple of weeks, I'll probably just go with the goose." He's apparently unaware that his brother Jim has been focusing on those same two species. Then he adds, "What's the deadline again? August 15? Wow. I better get on it."

The three competing Hautman brothers sometimes market themselves as the "Hautman Brothers" as opposed to three individual artists with three distinctive styles. The Hautman Brothers 2011 Wildlife Art Calendar, for example, includes work by all three brothers, as well as text promoting the three men, rather modestly, as "among America's foremost wildlife artists."

Collectively, the Hautman name—the brand, in modern marketspeak—has dominated the Federal Duck Stamp Contest like no other. That, as well as the notoriety that came with the Hautmans' pop culture exposure in the Coen brothers film *Fargo*, explains why no conversation about the recent history of the contest gets very far without some mention of at least one of them. (The *Fargo* reference was no fluke. The Coen brothers and the Hautman brothers grew up as childhood friends in St. Louis Park, Minnesota. Jim and Bob were living together at the time that the Coens were making the movie, and the filmmakers raided their studio while shooting. They took several paintings for the walls of the Gunderson home and Norm Gunderson's easel, as well as old brushes and paint supplies, mounted birds, and other things to use as props.)

But to overlook the personality differences among Jim, Bob, and Joe Hautman is to miss the subtle distinctions that make each one a fascinating study. In conversations with the three, as well as with oldest brother Pete, sister Amy, and their mother, Elaine, it quickly becomes clear that the family's three Federal Duck Stamp Contest winners were each shaped by unique wrinkles in their shared DNA.

For example, Pete, the writer, says that Bob's seemingly reckless approach to the onrushing 2010 contest deadline is typical. "I'll tell you a story about Bob," he begins, launching into a tale that he feels exemplifies Bob's headlong approach to just about everything he does, including sports.

Years ago, Pete says Bob used to play bandy, a cold-climate sport that's not for the faint of heart and has been around for at least two hundred years. Imagine a hockey rink the size of a regulation soccer field, patrolled by twenty-two players on ice skates who carry nasty hooked sticks. The object is to put a small orange ball into your opponent's net. You thought hockey was fast?

"Because the rink is so big, the skating tends to be very, very fast, because there's time to build up speed," Pete says.

During one such high-speed moment, Bob collided with another player, crushing one of his cheekbones. He was in tremendous pain. Pete recalls that "the doctor took a look at Bob's X-rays and said, 'What did you do the last time you broke your skull?'"

This, of course, was news to Bob. He hadn't realized he'd ever cracked his skull before—but Pete vividly remembers Bob's willingness to speculate. "Bob said, 'Well, it might have been the time I went through a windshield. Or it might have been the time I skateboarded down the stairs. Or'—and he went on and on. He'd had about four instances in his life when he might have broken his skull. But of course he never sought treatment."

This account jibes with one offered by Amy, also an artist,

who notes that Bob "has had more concussions and stitches than the rest of the family put together." She recalls that as a teenager Bob drove a baby blue Olds Cutlass that he called the "blue bullet." He'd customized it by painting flying ducks on it in green. One particular Halloween, Amy says, Bob outran the local cops in the car. At the time, he was "dressed as Beethoven in a teal paisley tuxedo and his long hair ratted on the top of his head."

Elaine Hautman describes Bob as having been a somewhat less than dedicated student who preferred practical jokes to academics. One time, she says, Bob decided to have some fun with his father, who'd often expressed skepticism about claims that Minnesota sometimes experienced "golf-ball-sized hail," that hoary cliché of TV meteorologists. On a stormy day, as their father sat inside with his newspaper near a window at the front of the family home, Bob organized some of his brothers to gather at the back of the house with several buckets of golf balls. They started chucking them over the roof. As the balls rained down on the roof and into the front yard, one brother ran inside shouting, "Golf-ball-sized hail! Golf-ball-sized hail!"

But dismissing Bob Hautman as carefree or even reckless as he approaches the 2010 Duck Stamp Contest deadline is to ignore the intense decision making going on inside his head—despite his claims to the contrary. While he may have been late putting brush to canvas, for months leading up to the August deadline he has been making a series of choices no less calculated than those being made by his intensely focused younger brother Jim. And in fact, Bob has now chosen as his subject the exact same species, the specklebelly goose.

Choosing the specklebelly already sets the two brothers apart from the field. Among the eventual 235 entries in the 2010 contest, more than 60 percent will feature the ubiquitous Canada goose or the colorful, absurd-looking northern shoveler. Blue-billed ruddy ducks will prove popular as well, accounting for more than 18 percent of the entries. The two Hautmans will number among the less than 13 percent of artists who decide to paint specklebellies. Only the relatively colorless and uncharismatic brant will prove less popular, representing just 8 percent of the entries.[1]

Although he downplays the significance of his pre-contest calculations, Bob has many of the same reasons for choosing the specklebelly as Jim. While he has no idea who will be on the judging panel in Berkeley, he has no doubt that the species is familiar to waterfowlers in the American West. "It's a guessing game," he says, "but the bird *is* a Western flyway bird."

Like Jim, Bob goes to the family friend's farm in New Germany to photograph the captive specklebelly geese there. But on his visit the geese are uncooperative and easily spooked. "They wouldn't come out in the sun, [and] I didn't get very good photos." But on a scouting trip to Shakopee, about forty minutes from his farm, he's pleasantly surprised when a pair of specklebellies fly in and land within range of his lens. He fires off about a hundred photos of the pair and hopes these will be enough to help him capture necessary details for his painting.

Back at the converted henhouse he uses as his studio, Hautman tries two initial poses—a single goose on the water and another solitary goose standing on terra firma. He eventually settles on the standing goose. But in choosing a background, he decides to paint in something that might give him an edge: a range of distinctly Western mountains. A friend in California has suggested a backdrop depicting the Sutter Buttes, a small and unusual volcanic range that rises from the floor of California's Sacramento Valley.[2] Western waterfowl enthusiasts know that the lakes around the Sutter Buttes are a magnet for migrating ducks and geese. Western judges. Western bird. Western scene. To Bob Hautman, as to his brother Jim, it seems like a good bet.

"I thought a Western scene would be good with the contest being judged in a Western state where there are thousands of white-fronted geese," he explains. "But the bottom line is you just have to do your best painting."

The only problem with calling Joe, Bob, and Jim Hautman "the New York Yankees of the Federal Duck Stamp Contest," as competitor Mark Berger does, is that it actually diminishes what the three sibling wildlife artists have accomplished during just two decades of duck-painting competition. True, the Yankees have won twenty-seven World Series titles and remain one of the most honored franchises in all of sports, but creating that record took the organization eighty-eight years, from its first title in 1921 to its most recent in 2009.[3]

The Hautman brothers began competing in the annual Duck Stamp Contest in the late 1980s. The first appearance of their family name among those of the top three finalists was in 1987, when Jim finished third in the competition for the 1988–1989 stamp. By the time 2010 rolled around, they had collectively won the federal contest a jaw-dropping eight times since Jim's first win in 1989.

At that pace, Team Hautman would win wildlife art's equivalent of the World Series approximately thirty-five times in the span it took the Yanks to win their twenty-seven titles.

The closer you look at the brothers' success record, the more impressive it becomes. For most duck stamp artists, a finish strong enough to qualify for the national tour (reserved for the top twenty-five to thirty point-getters each year) is the accomplishment of a lifetime. A finish among the top three can jump-start an art career, propelling a painter from hobbyist to professional overnight. A first-place win is an unparalleled career highlight and a ticket to every artist's fantasy life, in which their art can generate enough income to enable them to quit their day job and paint full-time.

During the twenty-two-year span between 1987 and 2009, a Hautman brother finished among the top three finalists sixteen times, including those eight wins, six second-place finishes, and two third-place finishes. Making that record statistically improbable is the contest rule, first enforced during the 1972 contest,[4] that makes winners ineligible to compete for the next three contests after their win. That means that all three Hautman brothers were eligible to compete together in only five contests during that period. In at least six of the contests, two of the three brothers were sitting it out.

Individual artists have achieved no-less-laudable records. Back in the days before winners were required to take a three-year hiatus after their victory, Iowa's Maynard Reece won the Federal Duck Stamp Contest a record five times between 1947 and 1970. Two artists have won it three times each, Virginian Edward Bierly (1955, 1962, and 1969) and Maryland's Stanley Stearns (1954, 1963, and 1965). Double winners include Edward Morris (1960 and 1961) and Minnesota's Leslie C. Kouba (1957 and 1966) and David Maass (1973 and 1981).

But despite their success, there doesn't seem to be the sort of toxic resentment toward the Hautmans that one might expect in a competition where the stakes are so high. Many artists who compete against the brothers, and others who know them, offer stories of pleasant encounters, kind words, and helpful advice from one Hautman or another.

"They're talented artists," says fellow Minnesota painter Bruce Miller, the 1992 Federal Duck Stamp Contest winner, whose work in wildlife art for years has been moving toward and incorporating elements of the Russian impressionism he so admires. "They've zeroed in on this thing as the main focus in their lives. And the three of them, they're smart guys. Shit, Joe used to be a physicist. So they've analyzed this thing down to the minutiae, and they have every little thing figured out. That's what they decided to do."

Even when Miller adds that "they're far from being the best artists in Minnesota," his words arrive without the sting of pettiness or jealousy. While he's closest to Bob, he considers all three brothers his friends.

Robert Bealle, who competed against the Hautmans for most of the twenty-seven years he quested after the prize before finally winning the federal contest in 2009, professes a deep and seemingly sincere respect for the brothers' talent. And Judy Geck, the visitor services librarian at the Minnesota Valley National Wildlife Refuge, just smiles when the Hautman name comes up.

Geck is the sole staffer one Sunday morning at the impressive visitor center of the fourteen-thousand-acre refuge, a marsh along the Minnesota River directly beneath the flight path of nearby Minneapolis/St. Paul International Airport, and just as close to the Mall of America. She says, "They're great role models, those guys are. They're just so personable and so interested in talking to the kids who are submitting art for the Junior Duck Stamp Contest."

Similarly, in the living room turned studio of his suburban home in Los Alamitos, California, aerospace engineer and Duck Stamp Contest competitor Mark Berger recalls the day he met one of the brothers at a wildlife art show in Redlands, California. Joe Hautman, who holds a doctorate in physics but abandoned academia in 1992 to pursue a career as a wildlife artist, was touring with his painting of two pintails that had won the 2007 contest. "Joe's the reason I got involved in this," recalls Berger, who began competing in the federal contest in 2008. "I had met some other duck stamp artists, but it wasn't until I met Joe that I thought the whole thing appealed to me, because he had this science background, and I just liked talking to him."

Just a few feet away from where he's sitting in his living room studio, Berger's respect for the fabled Hautmans is on full display. On his easel—along with various early-stage sketches, photo composites, and wing studies and the canvas upon which he is painting his 2010 contest entry of two airborne Canada geese—hangs a previous Duck Stamp Contest entry, two Canada geese painted by Jim Hautman.

"That's just up there as a reminder," Berger says. "It came in second two years ago, but that's the kind of quality I'm shooting for."

If you're looking for a point of origin to the Hautman story, you'll find a clue hanging above a marble-faced fireplace in the music room of Joe Hautman's five-thousand-square-foot mid-century-modern home in suburban Plymouth, Minnesota, just west of Minneapolis. An oil-on-canvas painting, probably done in the late 1940s or early 1950s, features five canvasbacks in flight. By today's hyperrealistic duck stamp standards, it's crude and ill proportioned—the birds too small, the landscape ambiguous, what looks like a misplaced and wispy shaft of wheat dominating the foreground. But it's obviously hung in a place of honor. The understated signature in the lower right corner reads simply, "Hautman."

"My dad painted it," Joe Hautman says with obvious pride.

Thomas "Tuck" Hautman, the family patriarch, who died in 1995, was untrained as an artist, although he did have a law degree and a brief legal career. He was far too busy helping support the seven Hautman children with the trailer-rental business he eventually created to spend much time at the easel. Joe says he's aware of only a few paintings by his father and a couple more that he painted with his wife, Elaine, after they were first married. All involved birds of some type, because, as everyone agrees, Tuck Hautman's true passion was not art, but ducks and duck hunting.

"For the amount he painted, he did a good job," Joe says. "This is the only one I've got."

Like Tuck, all three of his artist sons became passionate hunters, and they recall with reverence their father's collection of duck stamps. And the painting's prominence in Joe's home might suggest that the brothers' passion for the medium stems from some patriarchal gene. But in truth, that passion comes mostly from their mother, a lifelong artist who, at eighty-seven in the spring of 2010, lives in a residential facility with about 450 other seniors about a mile from Joe, and just a couple of miles from where he and his siblings grew up. Her extraordinary and eclectic paintings and drawings hang throughout Joe's house: a colorful abstract still life of nasturtiums, an homage to Vincent van Gogh showing the ear-bandaged Dutch impressionist smoking a pipe beside a table of fruit and flowers, and renditions of cave paintings featuring horses and plains animals.

The kids grew up painting, potting, and making messes of all kinds amid what middle child Amy recalls as "a bounty of art supplies . . . Art was always important in the Hautman household." It was during one of their mother's forays into the commercial art world that sons Jim and Bob first started painting waterfowl. Elaine had begun painting ducks on driftwood during a visit to her brother's cabin on Minnesota's Lake Vermilion, and a friend suggested that she sell the paintings at a Christmas boutique.

They sold well, "so I asked the kids if they wanted to paint some," Elaine says. "Theirs sold too. Jimmy and Bob were living together and painting houses at the time, and they were so happy about it. So they got old trees and made slices out of them and painted on them. They started making clocks and trivets and things and selling them in stores around Minneapolis. They made good money at it. Then they decided to enter the Duck Stamp Contest, and from then on they started painting ducks."

Perhaps it's not surprising that four of the seven siblings— Joe, Bob, Jim, and Amy—now make their living as professional artists. What *is* surprising is that only two of the seven actually studied art. Amy, now raising her own family and working as a professional fine arts painter in North Carolina, earned her bachelor of arts degree in studio arts and art history at the University of Minnesota. Pete attended the Minneapolis College of Art and Design but "got interested in other things" and now makes his living as a writer. He won the 2004 National Book Award for Young People's Literature for *Godless*, the story of a teenage boy who decides to invent a new religion, with his town's water tower as its deity.

Pete watched from the beginning as Joe, Bob, and Jim each set their sights on the grandest prize in the world of wildlife art, beginning with their entries in state contests. And he says he's struck again and again by their analytical approach to the Federal Duck Stamp Contest.

"If they're doing a painting of a great blue heron in the water, for example, it's fairly typical of the way most people approach representational painting," he says. "But they approach the duck stamp more like they're doing art for an ad campaign. It involves a lot of thinking about the needs and tastes of the judges. They show their duck stamp paintings to dozens of people. They want to know how the thing hits people emotionally, whether they're experienced artists or people who know nothing about art. They'll even do multiple versions—postures, different poses, different weather in the background. It's a very analytical and scientific approach."

Jim, the youngest, says the contest rules dictate that analytical approach. "I try to keep an open mind to start out with, but there's a real narrow parameter of what you can do that would have a chance. Within that, there's an infinite array of things. For instance, it has to be realistic. The bird has to be fairly large in the painting. There has to be nice color. There's a lot of things it just *has* to be. But within that, I like to try at least three rough sketches that are completely different, just to explore ideas."

And Jim agrees with those who say that he and his brothers are particularly good at eliminating potential negatives from their Duck Stamp Contest entries. Waterfowl feet, for example, are notoriously difficult for an artist to get right. And it's no coincidence that not a single specklebelly foot is visible on any of the three geese depicted in the two Hautman entries for 2010; in both paintings, the geese are standing in reeds that artfully obscure everything below a certain point on their legs.

"Keep in mind that I'm one of these guys who does overanalyze things," Jim says. "I get *Scientific American* for fun reading, so I definitely have a little bit of that. But the interesting thing about painting the duck stamp entry is that there are so many ways that you can ruin your chances. So that's one step, to just not do anything goofy that simply won't work."

He mentions another artist, a friend, who one year insisted on painting diving ducks swimming underwater. "Which is a cool idea, and he did a nice job with them, but it's hard enough to win the contest without one strike against you. That just falls under the category of things people haven't seen, things people can't relate to. I've seen it, but not very many other people have. So that's one of my main thoughts: to not do anything screwy. You don't want to do something that three people are gonna really like and two people are gonna hate. The judges will pick them apart, and they'll find reasons to deduct points from your painting."

In addition to that no-negatives instinct, the brothers share a competitive nature that apparently drives them to excel. To a man, they all deny trying to one-up their brothers, offering an all-for-one-and-one-for-all approach worthy of the Three

Musketeers. What's good for one Hautman is good for them all, yadda, yadda, yadda. True, they critique one another's work, just as they workshop their pieces by soliciting reactions from others they trust. But all three agree that their work improves because of that process.

The whole truth, however, is a bit more complicated.

The three brothers are intensely driven. While seeming laid-back in their movements and manner of speaking, Bob and Jim spent years exercising their competitive impulses on Minnesota's hockey rinks. Joe, with his doctorate in theoretical physics, excelled in the often cutthroat world of academia. They'll admit to nothing more than a friendly, familial approach to competition among themselves, but at times they'll let slip some evidence to the contrary.

Joe, for example, remembers family competitions involving everything from building towers out of toothpicks to drinking pineapple juice. Bob tells the story of the night about thirty years ago when the three of them engaged in an unusual contest. They were all living at home at the time, and they decided to see who could write the smallest. "What we started writing was 'Hi Joe. How are you?' Trying to write it smaller and smaller [but] so you could still read it."

The contest went on for hours. Eventually, Bob says, he got tired and went to bed. "It got to a certain point where I couldn't do it. It just got too small. But Jim and Joe got out the emery cloth, the finest, finest kind, and most all of their time was spent getting the pencil to such a small point. I think they were up until three in the morning."

When Bob got up the next day, he found scattered sheets of

paper that appeared to be covered in pencil lines. "But when you got the microscope on it, sure enough it said, 'Hi Joe. How are you?' You know those miniature artists who draw animals on a human hair and have to do their strokes between heartbeats and stuff? It was like that."

In art, the brothers' individual personalities manifest themselves in interesting ways, Pete says. "I think other perceptive wildlife artists can ID them from one another, because of their styles. They can look at [their work] and say, 'That's Jim. That's Bob. That's Joe.' Bob has a very different, gut-level approach, which gives his work a lot of life. Jim, when he holds a brush, he holds it very, very tightly—so tightly that he's had tendon problems. But when Bob paints, if you could reach over his shoulder and take the brush out of his fingers, he wouldn't even feel it. And where Jim might use a short brush with stiff bristles that give him ultimate control—Jim's backgrounds have as much detail as the animals do, almost painfully sharp—Bob would use a long, soft brush with soft bristles. You see it mostly in his non–duck-stamp paintings; they're more impressionistic."

Pete says he can see physical differences among the brothers manifested in their paintings as well. "Look at the animals in their paintings sometime and you'll see the extent to which they're doing self-portraits each time," he says.

Pete describes Jim as a mesomorph, "a fairly solid, muscular guy." As a result, he says, "Jim's paintings have a power to them," much like those of Minnesota native and 1987 Duck Stamp Contest winner Daniel Smith, now living in Montana, who in his early twenties won trophies for Best Chest and Most Muscular in the Mr. Minnesota bodybuilding competition.[5] By contrast, Pete says, Bob's paintings "have an *energy*. He's very,

very good with textures, and his paintings have a physicality to them."

Joe, on the other hand, "is more of an ectomorph," someone with a thinner, less muscular physique. And that's a fair description of the man who in April 2010 answers the door of his elegant Plymouth home.

Padding about his bright studio in standard gray sweats, fifty-three-year-old Joe Hautman asks a question almost as casually as he's dressed: "Do you know how big a hundred thousand is?"

He's wearing wire-rimmed eyeglasses and sporting a day's growth of beard on his thin and angular face. Unable to compete in the 2010 Federal Duck Stamp Contest because of his 2007 win, he has the luxury of not working toward the August 15 deadline on this spring afternoon. That means the physicist's formidable mind is free to wander. And it does.

"It kind of fascinates me sometimes trying to estimate large numbers, and how you can even conceive them," he says. "Because above a certain number, like a billion people, it's so hard. So I did this."

He produces a piece of paper that appears to be gray with a white border and lays it on his cluttered desk. "This is a hundred thousand dots." He pulls out another, similar page. "Here's twenty thousand dots."

"Actually," he continues, "I think how this got started is, you know when you're hunting or taking photos of ducks, and a flock goes by, you guess, 'There's fifty mallards in that flock'?"

To a scientist like Joe Hautman, guessing is a maddening exercise in imprecision. He moves to a nearby computer screen and calls up an image file called "Many Birds," which shows ducks in a clustered flight formation against an open sky. "Here's what fifty ducks looks like." He calls up an image of two hundred ducks. Then an image of a thousand.

Clearly, numbers matter to the oldest of the three Hautman Duck Stamp Contest winners. And that moment of casual free association underscores the assessment of many observers that Joe's is a remarkable and interesting mind. Stories abound.

Sister Amy swears that Joe is capable of reading a book and playing classical piano at the same time. "He doesn't do that as a regular thing, but he *can*," she says. "He's interested in the fact that his brain is wired that way." On the other hand, she also remembers the day when her "brilliant" brother was scheduled to attend his graduation ceremony after earning his bachelor's degree from the University of Minnesota. "I remember him standing in my parents' kitchen, holding his gold cords of distinction and saying, 'Oh! I forgot to go to commencement!' "

Applying a mind like that to the task of painting wildlife has produced interesting results—and, by 2010, three Federal Duck Stamp Contest wins.

"Joe can't do a painting unless there's something about it that's different than everything he's done before," says Pete. "He's looking for internal stimulation."

Pete says that his younger brother's restless search for intellectual inspiration manifested itself most dramatically when he decided to walk away from a successful career as a physicist in academia to pursue wildlife art full-time. Pete says that 1992 decision was consistent with the person he has known since Joe was born, and evidence of Joe's intense desire to do things well.

"When he was younger, he was always very good at what he did, whatever it was," Pete says. "But he also worked very, very hard to get good. He's kind of obsessive. When he was playing piano, he was constantly practicing. I never saw anybody practice free throws as hard as Joe did. He'd shoot five hundred free throws and probably hold the ball five hundred different ways. That's his problem with golf. Some people strive for consistency, but not him. He always believes things can be better, and it shows up in every aspect of his life."

Elaine Hautman sees Joe with the eyes of a mother who clearly remembers which of her kids gave her the fewest gray hairs. "He always sort of knew what to do next," she says. "He helped all the other kids, and he still does. When they have a problem with their computer or TV, they call Joe. He was always good at figuring things out." She adds that Joe is the only one of her wildlife artist sons who is comfortable with the public side of being a Duck Stamp Contest winner. "He doesn't mind. Teaching got him used to that."

Like Joe, Jim, her youngest, "just does what he's supposed to do. He's all-around good." Most Wednesdays, she says, Jim shows up for lunch and to paint with her, everything from still lifes to each other. "They're trying to get me to paint more because I have neuropathy in my hands," she adds. "It's an old-age thing."

She concedes that all three of her contest-winning sons are terrible salesmen. In that respect, she says, all three take after her. "They don't like having shows. They say they get stuck talking to someone, and it's hard to break away. They just don't like it."

That reluctance to be the center of attention—that essential Minnesota-ness so deftly conveyed by Garrison Keillor in his

*Prairie Home Companion* show, with its fictional Lake Wobe-gon—is what keeps the family matriarch from competing against her three sons in the Federal Duck Stamp Contest. "They keep telling me I should enter, but I don't think I'd enjoy it. I wouldn't mind doing the painting, and I've thought of it a few times, but all the speaking and stuff . . ."

# THE ANNUAL ORDEAL OF ARTISTIC CHOICES

THROUGH THE SPRING and summer of 2010, in every corner of the pro-am competitive-duck-painting universe, the 235 wildlife artists who plan to compete in the upcoming Federal Duck Stamp Contest are making a series of educated but often pointless guesses about what the judges might want. And the more you talk to the artists who compete, the more they remind you of baseball players whose adherence to inviolable pregame routines and superstitions—refusing to step on the foul line or to shave during a hitting streak, for example—is a nod to whatever mysterious forces they believe control their fate.

Both find comfort in the illusion of control.

Why else would so many artists spend so much time and energy speculating? To recap, duck stamp paintings are judged anonymously, in the order in which they've been submitted, and by an entirely different panel of five judges each year, whose names are not announced until the day the contest judging begins. Each of those judges carries out their mission using their own aesthetic sensibilities, based on their background in art, conservation, politics, outdoorsmanship, or whatever other field they've been drawn from. Trying to predict what the judges will choose in any given year is like trying to predict earthquakes or read the future in scattered chicken bones. But every year, most competing artists try.

In addition, duck stamp artists compete against opponents whose names they may not know and whose work they cannot see until after they've finished their own entry. They simply have no idea whether they've chosen a species that by sheer numbers will quickly seem stale to the judges, or how, for example, their Canada goose painting will compare to the eighty-three other Canada goose paintings that eventually will be entered in the 2010 contest. Many artists try to divine likely duck stamp trends from the previous year's entries, an almost always futile exercise. One contest watcher recalls a year when one of the judges was known to be an avid decoy collector. Because the winning painting that year included a decoy, the following year's field included more than the usual number of paintings featuring decoys. The artists who made that choice did so, of course, even though that particular judge would not be on the panel judging their entry.

Logic has nothing to do with it.

It's the same with the rituals and routines of individual artists. California's Sherrie Russell Meline, whose 2005-winning painting ended up on the 2006–2007 stamp and made her only the second female Federal Duck Stamp Artist, paints late at night with her TV tuned to Fox News. Why? It's just her thing. She also tries to postmark her entry by August 1, about two weeks before the August 15 deadline. When she misses her superstitious, self-imposed deadline by a few days in 2010, she worries about it as she finally puts her portrait of a nesting Canada goose in the mail.

Adam Grimm, whose win in 1999 when he was just twenty-one made him the youngest winner in Federal Duck Stamp Contest history, displacing Jim Hautman, tries to time sending his entry each year to place it in the middle group of arrivals rather than among the first or last entries. He claims with unshakable certainty, "It's been shown that the judges are more likely to put your painting through if it's from the middle of the pack. But getting into the middle of the group is hard to do. It's, like, a whole science."

Bruce Miller is running out of time. It's less than three weeks before the August 15 deadline to enter the contest that he simply calls "the Federal."

The self-taught artist, a rugged former Eagle Scout, musician, and building contractor, has just returned home to the woodsy, upscale Minneapolis suburb of Mound from a three-week trip to Calgary, Alberta, where he engaged in the necessary ritual of being an "artist," which has nothing to do with painting and everything to do with hawking his paintings at a public show. He's scheduled for another trip on August 6; by his calculation, he has only four working days to create his 2010 Duck Stamp Contest entry.

His victory in the 1992 contest changed his life—his rustic five-thousand-square-foot home on the shore of Lake Minnetonka testifies to that—but he's had a long winless streak since then, six years longer than Jim Hautman's twelve-year drought. Even though his artistic ambitions have driven him into other realms—that profound appreciation of Russian impressionism, for example—he returns year after year to compete in the Federal because he knows better than most how lucrative a win can be. "I do one highly detailed painting a year," he says, "and that's the Federal Duck Stamp . . . I do it strictly for the money, just because it's a financial opportunity."

Like most of his competitors, Miller is focusing on what will prove to be the two most popular species in the 2010 contest, the Canada goose and the northern shoveler. He has decent reference photos of each that he shot with his ancient 35mm Nikon D70. In May, he spotted a pair of nesting Canada geese near his home and imagined reworking a piece he'd done previously called *Standing Guard*, which shows a hen sitting on a nest while her mate stands protectively in front of her. In late July, though, he changed his mind. The shoveler was haunting him.

Three times before, he'd entered a painting of a shoveler pair, a drake and a hen, and twice it had done well. The first time, in 2004, it tied for third with a painting of a Ross's goose by Sherrie Russell Meline and ended up in fourth place after the tie-break vote. Two years later, in 2006, a reworked version placed second to Meline's reworked Ross's goose. Certain he was close, he reworked it again for the 2008 contest, but while it did finish among the top twenty, the judges that year didn't even advance it to the final round. Miller is convinced that he "watered it down to the point where it was just absolutely pretty boring."

But he can't let it go.

"What I'm gonna do is—I have a very dynamic shot of a drake shoveler. It's one of the most spectacular colored birds that you'll see in the spring, when it's in full plumage. It has to do with the contrast and the white breast and the orangish-rust side feathers and then the black head. But the hardest part about shovelers is that they're goofy-looking birds. So you have to somehow make a goofy-looking bird look good."

His plan: While hewing to the contest's strict demands for

anatomical accuracy, he will paint his single drake shoveler in profile, in a way that downplays the duck's absurd, shovel-like bill. But he's worried about one X factor with the shoveler that has nothing to do with its appearance. It tastes as weird as it looks, or at least that's how some hunters feel. Like the two Hautman brothers against whom he'll be competing, he knows that it takes only one judge for whom a shoveler has a negative connotation to turn the tide against entries depicting that bird.

Still, in Miller's mind, the issue is finally settled. He's going for the shoveler.

"I want to take a chance," he says. "There's gonna be a ton of geese this year. I don't want it to look like everybody else's design."

For many competitors, especially those who have known the financial benefits of a win, such gymnastic attempts to predict the future are more than just superstitious exercises. "For people who know they have a serious competitive entry and a shot at winning, it's a lot of stress," says thirty-one-year-old Adam Grimm, who with his wife, Janet, is raising two young daughters in Union County, South Dakota, in the spring of 2010. "I know I'm going to put in a lot of serious effort and really commit to this, and if it doesn't win, I might have to forgo a new roof on the house, or this or that. Where if you do win, you *can* do this or that. My wife actually talked to me about having another baby. But financially it's like . . . maybe if I win the Federal this year. The judges have no knowledge of any of this, but the effect it has on people's lives is extraordinary."

Grimm paints his Duck Stamp Contest entries in oils, rather than the faster-drying acrylic paints preferred by most of the other artists, and so by the end of May 2010 his entry is well under way. He's already somewhat legendary for the extent of his field research—the hunter and outdoorsman moved from Ohio to South Dakota so he could be closer to the migratory flyways of American waterfowl. And he has spent much of the previous two months in the field, using decoys and live recordings of birds played through his iPod to lure birds close enough for him to take reference photographs. By mid-May, he had narrowed down his options to three: the northern shoveler, the specklebelly, and the Canada goose.

Grimm's instincts told him that the Canada goose was likely to be the most common species entered, and he believes that the judges seldom favor the most-entered bird. He ruled that one out first. And despite his best efforts, he'd been unable to get any great reference photos for specklebellies through March and April. So that was out. "The shoveler was the only species left," he recalls. "They don't come until later in the migration, and I was getting nervous."

He imagined a painting featuring two shovelers, a drake and a hen, in flight. He knew that his chances of getting just the right photograph of two birds together were slim, so, like many artists, he'd need to piece together multiple images in Photoshop to get the composition he wanted. He repainted some of his decoys to look like shovelers, and one day he dialed the iPod to his shoveler recordings and settled into a flooded cornfield to wait.

It worked. "I had flock after flock coming in," he says. The wind and light cooperated as well, and by day's end he had about a thousand photos he could dissect and piece together to create the composition he was imagining.

So Grimm began to paint, and he did so with confidence,

having mocked up a detailed version of the portrait in Photoshop, sweating its many fine points during the planning stage rather than during the painting process. Plus, regardless of how the painting fares in the contest, he has already agreed to sell the original to one of his regular collectors for enough money to make it worth his time. And if it wins the Duck Stamp Contest, the original sale agreement will be voided, and bidding will begin among several interested clients.

These are the kinds of advantages that accrue to a previous winner.

By the time Grimm is done with his entry in late July, the airborne shovelers look almost exactly as he designed them in the photoshopped mock-up, with the mottled brown hen in the background and the colorful, green-headed drake in the foreground, its right wing spooning almost protectively over the airborne hen. Beneath the birds, he has opted for a marsh rather than a cornfield, with a tiny little muskrat nest sprouting almost imperceptibly from the water and a windmill and a red-roofed barn on the horizon. Above them, he has adjusted the backdrop to include just the right balance of gray clouds and blue sky.

"Some of my friends looked at it and thought it was my best work to date," he says about two weeks before putting it in the mail. "Of course, that doesn't matter, because it's all up to the judges."

The contest's unpredictability leaves both seasoned competitors such as Grimm and newbies such as Mark Berger to grapple alone with paint boxes, brushes, and easels, as well as their assumptions, their hunches, and—in the spring of 2010—seventy-six years of historical precedent.

Like many artists, Berger has been planning his 2010 entry since the previous October, when the 2009 contest judging ended. He has chosen his favorite from among the five eligible species and has even made the critical decision to gamble on two birds in the air, which many artists say is among the most difficult poses to get right. He decided he liked the odds.

To an aerospace engineer such as Berger, or a former physicist such as Joe Hautman, or other artists who are similarly wired, the world is a numbers game, a reassuring calculus in which, if you adjust for the X factors, the outcome is predetermined. People like that find something affirming, almost holy, in the beautiful certainty of math.

Berger's home in Los Alamitos, an Orange County bedroom community just south of Los Angeles, is not far from the facilities where for more than three decades he has made his name as an engineer for aerospace companies such as Hughes, Rockwell, McDonnell Douglas, and Boeing. His fine analytical mind and knack for details served him well on programs such as the space shuttle, the International Space Station, and the Delta III rocket. But in 2003, Berger began painting as a hobby, and he pursued his passion methodically.

He began painting his kids, his wife, Pacific seascapes. In May 2008, he decided to enter one of his seascape paintings in a local art contest, at the nearby Sunset Beach Art Festival. It was the first art contest he'd ever entered, and his painting of the Seal Beach strand not far from his home won the Best in Show award. In addition to that confidence booster, Berger began to understand that his art might have more tangible value. That same year, for example, he was able to trade two of his paintings for a twelve-year-old Infiniti Q45 for the older of his two sons.

Berger had spent years coaching youth sports leagues in Los Alamitos, where he and his family have lived since 1989. As his younger son prepared to leave for college and he and wife Kathy faced an empty nest, Berger had a conversation with two artists he'd met at local art shows, Federal Duck Stamp Contest veterans Robert Richert and Robert Copple. They told him about the contest, about the fantastic amounts of money at stake, and about the allure of the national wildlife-art competition.

Unfortunately, Berger had no particular interest in painting ducks. But he did find the notion of painting ducks as a sport compelling. The former baseball player's competitive instincts took over. He told himself he'd enter the contest for three years. Worst-case scenario, he figured, the hundreds of hours he'd spend at his easel to create his duck paintings would make him a better painter. Best-case scenario: He'd somehow crack the code, master the mystifying calculus of aesthetics, and prevail in this strange new world.

Berger approached the 2008 Federal Duck Stamp Contest with an athlete's intense focus. The fifty-five-year-old Pittsburgh native had learned to compete in high school while playing football, basketball, and baseball. He'd been a standout shortstop at Central Catholic High School and a walk-on baseball talent at Penn State, where he'd studied mechanical engineering. He'd later had two tryouts with the Pittsburgh Pirates.

That first year, his floating Canada goose washed out in the first round. Among the five judges that year, only two thought Berger's goose worthy of advancing to the second round, which left his entry one vote short of the three "In" votes it needed to move on.

Undaunted, Berger recommitted himself to the task. Even

then, the contest's reputation as a potential ticket to financial independence was fueling his fantasies about someday retiring from his day job to paint full-time. To prepare for his 2009 entry, he began frequenting small, public Willow Park in nearby Cypress on a mission that would bring him back to the park at least fifteen times in the winter of 2008, always with his camera and a sack of birdseed to lure the waterfowl that wintered there. "I figured I could spend ten thousand dollars on a big lens," he recalls, "or ten dollars on a bag of seed."

By the time he was ready to begin painting, Berger had studied the recent history of the contest and noticed what he considered to be clues to victory. For example, the 2008 winner had come from among the early submissions, so Berger decided to time the mailing of his 2009 entry accordingly. How would you rather have your duck judged? he thought. By jaded judges who were tired after viewing more than two hundred duck paintings, or among entries presented to still-fresh judges early in the process? (Among the 224 entries that year, Berger's was Entry No. 31.)

His critical analysis didn't stop there. He made a science of studying past winners, determining, for example, that in many of the winning paintings, the background horizon was about one sixth of the way up from the bottom of the scene. After a bicycling accident laid him up for a few weeks in spring 2009, making it impossible to paint, he spent his downtime analyzing the duck stamp equivalent of game films.

"I went through and studied the winners [on the Duck Stamp Program's website]," Berger recalls. His conclusions? "Two birds is definitely better than one." Birds in flight, compared with birds floating on a pond, seemed more dynamic and might impress the judges.

One of the eligible ducks for 2009 was a wigeon, which has patches of bright green plumage on its head and wings. He settled on that duck because it's common in Southern California, and he knew he could take a lot of reference photographs. In addition to his one-sixth horizon revelation, he also concluded that simple designs were better, because something too busy would not translate well when the painting was reduced to stamp size.

"I just tried to look for basic things to put mine in the ballpark," he says.

Through the summer and into October 2009, right up to the week of the judging, Berger studied the other entries after the Duck Stamp Program posted all 224 on an affiliated website. He pored over a color printout of his fellow competitors' paintings—his handicapping sheets. Using the conclusions he'd made during his weeks of studying the contest data, he took a pen and systematically struck through the entries he thought were unlikely to survive the first round. He selected forty-one that he thought might represent the toughest competition, and he culled that list down to the strongest nine, including his among them. At that point, he calculated, he had about a 10 percent chance of becoming the next Federal Duck Stamp Artist.

Engineering and sports are very different than art, of course, and while Berger was attracted to the idea of beating the Hautmans at the game they dominated, he also was stepping into a world where comforting and precise rules don't necessarily apply.

He learned that hard lesson in 2009. After 130 hours at the living room easel, his Duck Stamp Contest entry for that year, his second attempt, was ready. He'd clearly followed the advice of one past winner to "paint the heck out of the duck" and let the rest of the painting support the lead bird. He had produced a well-composed, nicely detailed acrylic painting of two American wigeon in flight over an autumn marsh (actually, a lake at El Dorado Park in nearby Long Beach), the green-faced drake in the foreground, the less colorful hen in the background. The scene was a composite grafted together from a couple dozen digital photographs Berger had taken—a wing from one, a retracted foot from another. The basic composition of two birds in flight came from a single photograph.

The 2009 contest judging took place on a rainy October weekend at the Patuxent Research Refuge, in Laurel, Maryland. For a gathering of people focused on duck paintings, the general mood was serious and intense, despite absurdities such as the ritual playing of "Disco Duck" as part of the ceremonies, fake-waterfowl dioramas on either side of the judging table, and an angry-looking stuffed Canada goose appended to a reed-festooned podium.

For the most part, the faithful ignored the displays that offered a chance to stroke skunk and raccoon pelts or hold genuine animal skulls. More interesting, it seemed, were the paintings themselves, and the wares of Donald Leonard, a vendor from Florida who was peddling embroidered versions of duck stamps dating back to the contest's early years. As usual, the room was abuzz with supposed Hautman sightings.

Like Berger, some artists had traveled a long way to see how their duck would fare in head-to-head competition. And once Berger was there, all of his pre-contest handicapping seemed useless. As he perused his rivals the day before the judging, the control he had imagined he exercised over the outcome started to seem like one of Wonderland's illusions. Doubt crept into his voice as he assessed his chances.

"Winning depends on the subjective whims of five judges who change every year," he said. "So to get into this with the sole purpose of winning is a little bit crazy. It's a tremendous amount of work, and even if you produce a really nice piece, there's still gotta be some luck."

Amid the whispering in the small, dark auditorium, Berger tensed as the judges considered Entry No. 31, his wigeon. Everyone eyed the big, unforgiving screen where the fate of each painting flashed. By a 3–2 vote, his painting was "In." His ducks would advance to the next round.

Still, he realized that his estimated 10 percent chance of winning was probably optimistic. Disappointed but also pleased with his progress from the previous year's first-round knockout, he immediately set to work analyzing the vote tallies. And as he studied them, he grew perplexed. The numbers were confusing. "One judge had 18 paintings that he picked 'In' yesterday out of 224," he said. "The guy on the far right voted 113 'In.' That's a really strange disparity."

The judging the next day would be more nuanced. Each judge would assign a score of between one and five to each painting, with twenty-five being a perfect score. Only the top scorers would go to the final round. That night, between the first and second rounds, Berger savored the delicious anticipation of knowing that, in the wild and unpredictable world of competitive duck painting, anything could happen.

The problem with something so wild and unpredictable, of course, is that it's hard to parse the results. On that dreary Saturday in October 2009, only eight entries made it through to the final round—the top five scorers, including ties. Berger's wigeon finished with sixteen points, only two points behind one of the two competing Hautmans, but well out of the running. Like the *American Idol* contestant who makes it into the top ten, he finished high enough to be part of the national tour, high enough to spark a steaks-and-wine celebration with friends that night. "A hundred thousand people might see my painting," he said later, conceding that his year-two "minimum goal" had been to make it into the traveling exhibition.

The coveted Federal Duck Stamp Artist title went to fifty-seven-year-old Maryland farmer Robert Bealle. His painting showed a single, stationary, oddly monochromatic wigeon floating among some reeds. Berger might have been right about the wigeon being a good choice that year, and his theory about the advantages of early submission had survived intact (Bealle's entry was No. 50). But his pre-contest calculations about the appeal of multiple ducks and birds in flight lay in smoking ruins.

"I came here thinking I had a small chance to win, so I was a little disappointed when I realized I wasn't going to," he said. "But I'm happy I got this far." And he found reason to be encouraged during his post-finals analysis. He was convinced "the judges saw more attributes in mine the second time they saw it. It means I'm on the right track."

Even before he left the venue, Berger had resolved to take a crack at a pair of Canada geese in the 2010 contest. He already had figured out the time of day he wanted to depict, as well as the pose. "The painting I did last year had really nice lighting, but not sufficient skill. Now I'm a little further along on the skill."

But as he thought about the 2010 contest, the engineer realized that there remained a vast divide between those enterprises that were governed by precise rules and those that weren't. During his struggle across that divide, he felt, he had learned some valuable lessons.

"It's very unpredictable, in a relative sense, compared to engineering, so it doesn't make a lot of sense if you're just doing it for the purpose of winning."

Not all of his analysis was for naught. "The top three entries were in my list of the top forty-one. I was able to pick those out. So I can't control everything, but it's possible to predict what might be good enough to win. To be a finalist, that's about as much as I can control." In the end, he said, "If you say it's futile to try to win because it's so unpredictable, I say it also means I can win because it *is* so unpredictable."

After two years in the competitive-duck-painting arena, after getting stomped in 2008 and finishing better during the 2009 contest, the rocket scientist didn't see the pond as half empty, but half full. And so, lessons learned, Berger flew home to his easel in Southern California to start thinking about his third-year entry. For 2010, he had some geese to paint.

Two months before the 2010 contest's August deadline, Berger is 30 hours into a painting of two airborne Canada geese that he predicts, rather precisely, will take him 120 hours to finish.

The easel in his living room is studded with photographs and paintings of Canada geese on the wing, in addition to the Jim Hautman painting of the same species from which he is drawing inspiration.

Just getting his painting that far involved as much elaborate buildup as launching one of the rockets Berger had helped build. In addition to his various photo expeditions, he spent hours assembling his reference photos into rough composites that allowed him to tinker with how he wanted to stage the scene. When he had a selection of twenty-one workable possibilities, he emailed them to nearly fifty friends and fellow artists, soliciting their feedback and inviting them to "mix and match any bird or combination of birds with any background." He included composites of geese in flight, on water, and on land. He included some with a lone goose and others with pairs of geese. He included geese with only a single tree as a backdrop, geese over a lake, geese wading on a pond, geese with cattails in the foreground. As the feedback rolled in, he compiled what he considered to be the six best choices into a document, and vote totals and comments into a spreadsheet. Then he circulated those too.

At the end of the process, he concluded that the best design showed two geese flying over a lake, with muted fall foliage in the distant background, puffy gray-white clouds in a blue sky, the birds not touching, no cattails. Based on a reference photo, he painted his lead bird's webbed feet coming down, which gave them an unusual prominence in the frame.

By late July, more than a hundred hours into his effort— about twenty hours of that spent stretched out on a mattress on his living room floor because of back pain—he's fixing subtle inconsistencies in the line patterns of the birds' feathers and mulling over a possible flaw pointed out by his friend and fellow Duck Stamp Contest competitor Robert Copple earlier that week: a possible missing primary flight feather on the right wing of his lead goose.

The whole thing puts him in a bad mood. On the one hand, Copple has pointed out a potential flaw in his painting that could derail its chances if one of the judges decides to obsess about it. On the other, with the deadline just two weeks away and the painting so close to being finished, Berger is reluctant to change anything. "It appeals to me as it is. So what if a feather is missing?"

In the end, before he flies off to Washington, D.C., for a business trip—a trip that will give him the chance to hand-deliver his 2010 entry to the Duck Stamp Program's Arlington offices—he concludes that there is no missing feather and decides to leave the painting as it is.

But there's still one troubling X factor for which he can't account. "It all comes down to it being compared to something else, and I don't know what that something else is yet."

# THE POWER OF THE PRIZE

THE DAY THE world changed for Scot Storm began with a fight. He uses the word with some hesitation; like many Minnesotans, Storm tends to be private, polite, and reserved. The first time he tells the story, he calls it a "conversation." But when he tells it a second time, he lets the word slip. He and his wife, Kris, had a "fight" that morning.

Who could blame them? Four years earlier, they had taken a gamble familiar to many entrepreneurial couples. Storm was a successful architect, specializing in public education projects. He earned a good living, but something was missing. His true passion was painting, and the lifelong outdoorsman had become an accomplished wildlife artist even as he'd built his architecture career. In 2000, when he was thirty-eight, Storm and his wife took a grand leap of faith: Storm decided to become a full-time artist.

They had some savings as a financial cushion. Kris agreed to become his shipping clerk, booking agent, and general partner in the enterprise to give her husband time to paint. "My art career then was a hunt-and-peck system," Storm says. "We were trying all sorts of different shows. We probably did eighteen to twenty a year, from setting up in the local bank lobby to the trade shows across the country. We were trying a little bit of everything to find a niche."

By 2003, the money was running out, and tensions around the house were rising. They had twins by then, and for the first time they began to question whether or not they could still afford to pursue his dream.

"We were down on our luck as far as income," Storm recalls. "Kris wanted to go get a job. We had twins who were just a couple of years old. Her working with me allowed her to work at home, but the conversation was 'Who's going to get a part-time job to keep us on this path a little while longer?' We'd been doing a lot of shows, putting a lot of money into it, and it's pretty easy to get into debt. We didn't know how much longer we could sustain that."

The conversation that morning didn't end well. Storm was scheduled to show his work in Omaha, Nebraska, that week and needed to get on the road. He loaded his paintings, prints, and other supplies into a trailer and left the house upset and confused, the discussion unresolved. For the next two hours, he drove in a tunnel of dark thoughts. Maybe it was time to give up the dream.

Then his cell phone rang.

"It was the people from the Federal Duck Stamp Contest, telling me I'd made the finals," Storm says. The organizers wanted him to know that final judging was under way and a winner would be announced later that day. "I'd been a finalist before, and I was excited, but Kris and I had had such a disagreement, I just said, 'What am I doing? This isn't worth it. I need to get home and figure things out.'"

About 120 miles into the trip, he turned the trailer around.

When he arrived home two hours later, he and his wife resumed their conversation. They were still talking when his phone rang again. It was the Duck Stamp Contest organizers calling with the news that his painting of two redheads in flight had been chosen as the competition winner.

In that instant, Scot Storm's world changed forever. "We knew right away we were going to get some operational capital. I tell people it was my worst and my best day. It was like the closing of my career, and in the same day it was there again. For a long time I could never tell people that story. But without that moment I doubt that I would still be in the art world."

The days when winning the Federal Duck Stamp Contest practically guaranteed the Federal Duck Stamp Artist a million dollars or more—through the sale of limited-edition prints of the winning painting, licensing fees, and other such sources—are over, for reasons as varied as the decline in the number of hunters and collectors and the dwindling market for limited-edition duck stamp prints. And from all apparent evidence during the 2010 contest year, reigning and past Federal Duck Stamp Contest winners still can move freely about the streets without having to hire private security.

Winners certainly are mobbed by fans at the three big public duck stamp events each year—the Junior Duck Stamp Contest judging in April, the federal contest first-day-of-sale ceremonies in June, and the federal contest finals in October—and their signatures and remarques on stamps, prints, and other ephemera impart real value in the peculiar universe of duck stamp collectors and aficionados.

But things have definitely changed—a modern reality that worries those who revere the program and are concerned about its future.

Mount Shasta, California, artist Sherrie Russell Meline was lured into the competition in 1985 because she saw it as a way to prove herself as an artist. "For me, it was the challenge of it, to compete with the best in the country," she says. "And to be recognized as a leading waterfowl artist is a neat thing, because there've only been seventy-five artists who have been selected. It becomes part of the archives of American history. To be part of something that big, and yet it's such a small group of people, that was an attractive thing."

But, Meline concedes, it was hard to ignore what was happening in the duck stamp world at the time. Since the early 1970s, the market for limited-edition duck stamp prints had been steadily rising, with prints of the winning Duck Stamp Contest painting in increasingly high demand.[1] Add an artist's signature to one of those prints and the value multiplied. While studying fine art at the University of Wisconsin, from which she graduated with honors in 1972, Meline had started collecting duck decoys at barn and yard sales "as an inexpensive way to decorate my college apartment." By 1980, at which point she was living amid the natural splendor of Mount Shasta, her interest in waterfowl had begun to deepen.

"A group of us were putting together a Christmas craft fair here in Mount Shasta, and I was asked to contribute. We needed someone to do men's gifts, and I got elected. I thought, 'Well, I always liked ducks. I'll do some duck things.'"

At the time, her idea of a duck was pretty limited. "Mallards and white ducks with orange bills, the little domestic things—that's what I thought ducks were. I had no clue what else was out there in the world." She bought an Audubon field guide and thumbed through it. "I had only collected mallard decoys, because I recognized them. So I was really shocked once I started researching and found out there were many different species."

Intrigued, one fall day she gathered up her field guide and her young son Scott for the ninety-minute drive to the Lower Klamath National Wildlife Refuge, near Tule Lake. "I just drove up in the afternoon to go see what the birds really looked like. It was fun. I'd seen these drawings in this little Audubon book. Then to see the real birds out there, it was very interesting. I guess it's how birders react when they see a yellow-bellied sapsucker or whatever. Ooh, that's a gadwall! That's a shoveler! It was exciting. It really did get my interest, because the colors were incredible."

At that point, she'd never heard of a duck stamp. That revelation came in Sacramento in 1982, at the Pacific Flyway Decoy Association's annual wildlife art show. She was painting ducks on pieces of wood at the time. They'd sold well at the Mount Shasta craft show, so she'd decided to see if she could make some money at a "real duck show."

She says she "bombed" while peddling her paintings in the show's crowded vendor area. Undaunted, the following year she submitted more traditional paintings on paper and canvas to the jury charged with choosing artists for the show. The jury invited her to show her paintings in a more exclusive area with established wildlife artists—what she calls "the big guys"—and she even sold a few pieces. That's where she met fellow California wildlife artist Robert Steiner, who told her about the Federal Duck Stamp Contest. She entered California's duck stamp competition in 1984, and the following year she entered a painting in the federal contest.

Everything had changed in late 1979, when writer Sam Iker had published a story in the December–January issue of the widely circulated *National Wildlife* magazine titled "The World's Richest Art Competition?" In that story, Iker recounted how recent winners of the Federal Duck Stamp Contest had become rich almost overnight and how one artist's bank account had swelled by $450,000 as a result of his win, a sum later noted as being four times larger than the cash award for the Nobel Prize.

The gold rush was on.

Until then, the number of entries in the annual federal contest had reliably hovered around three hundred. But the following year, in 1980, nearly fourteen hundred artists entered. The year after that, more than fifteen hundred took their chances. By 1982, nearly twenty-one hundred duck painters had decided to enter the chase, a record high.[2] Because there was no entry fee, the contest had taken on a state lottery vibe. A professional artist's reputation and track record were no advantage in a contest where the paintings were submitted without signatures and the judges had no idea which artist's work they were judging. Before the entry fee was imposed after the 1982 contest, schoolteachers were having their students paint ducks as part of class projects, then entering those paintings en masse. While the judges made fairly quick work of separating the unsophisticated efforts of schoolchildren from those of artists with more advanced skills, the sweepstakes mentality prevailed. By the time Meline first entered in 1985, the fee had helped reduce the number of competitors to about fifteen hundred a year.

"Back then they used to call it the million-dollar duck," she says. "That's changed immensely, but back then that's the way it was. And the notoriety!"

Minnesota's Bruce Miller also noticed the growing public interest in wildlife art. Born in 1952, the onetime Eagle Scout had traveled an uncertain professional path. He'd been a musician, then a pressman for a printing company, and in 1976 he started a small but successful construction operation. Through it all, he painted.[3] An avid outdoorsman, he discovered the financial lure of wildlife art after one of his paintings sold as an auction item at a Ducks Unlimited banquet, earning him two hundred dollars. He started focusing his painting efforts on ducks, geese, and game, and his reputation, and sales, grew. In 1984, he did a limited-edition printing of one of his paintings, which showed a snowy owl standing on a frozen Lake Superior, and sales were so good that by the following year, he'd left his construction business behind.

Competing in the Federal Duck Stamp Contest was a logical next step. Like Meline, he'd heard the stories.

"I think the [money] actually peaked out with the guy who won it with a cinnamon teal in 1984," he says, referring to artist Gerald Mobley's winning 1984 entry for the 1985–1986 stamp. "I heard he grossed $2.2 million in print sales." (Mobley, a modest Oklahoman, calls that number "overblown" but does concede that his publisher once estimated post-win limited-edition sales at $1.8 million. "I didn't *make* that, of course," Mobley says, noting the necessary promotional travel, advertising, and other overhead costs. He also suggests that William Morris's fiftieth-anniversary stamp painting the year before actually generated more money.)

"After that, it started to lose momentum, and it's been on a slow decline ever since," Miller says. "But [they] hit it right at the absolute pinnacle of the wildlife art, and especially the duck stamp craze."

Miller is referring to the wildlife art "frenzy" of the late 1980s that made possible his financial success. As he speaks, he's seated in the upstairs studio of his expansive home on Lake Minnetonka, which he shares with his wife, a fourteen-year-old daughter, an eleven-year-old son, and a nuzzling and worshipful black Lab named Gus whose skills in a duck blind Miller describes in equally worshipful terms. "You had everybody and his brother jumping out of the woodwork opening wildlife galleries, you had all these banquets, people running up huge editions of prints, and it basically became oversaturated."

Miller says that the market for paper prints was still lucrative when he won the federal contest in 1992, but that by the mid-1990s it had started to crash. "Like I say, the greed factor, in my mind, kicked in with these publishers doing unlimited prints and huge editions, and so the stuff just wasn't as collectible as it had been earlier, when people had more integrity as far as keeping edition sizes smaller so these prints were actually collectible," he says. "But it was much the same as any other industry. I mean, people jump in on it. The paper-print market was like printing money because it was so cheap to print. And I'm not just talking about the duck stamp; I'm talking about prints across the board. You could do an edition of a thousand prints, for example, and if you amortize the thing out into your publishing costs, they'd cost you two or three bucks apiece. You might sell them for a hundred or hundred fifty dollars retail, or even seventy-five dollars wholesale, but you're still making a lot of money."

A cynic might compare the scramble to cash in on the craze to the excesses of the market hunters of the late nineteenth and twentieth centuries. Miller makes no apologies for chasing the dream.

"When I won it in '92, it was still worth a *lot* of money," he says. "I mean, you can't complain about what it's worth now, because it's still worth a fair amount of money. But it pales in comparison to what it was worth back then."

Miller offers another example of the high stakes and high pressure in previous years. One of his artistic role models, fellow Minnesotan Phil Scholer, won the federal contest in 1982 with a pair of pintail ducks on a placid pond. While Scholer said the win was the highlight of his art career, he also found that the resulting spotlight "changed the way people related to me and vice versa," which, along with the demands of handling his art business during the year after his victory, he found "very stressful."[4]

"Phil's an interesting guy, and really, really talented," Miller says. "He won the 1982 contest and made a ton of money. But after he won the Federal, he decided to publish the [prints] himself. From a business standpoint, it was too stressful. He probably painted for another five years after winning the Federal, and produced some really nice paintings, but he just burned out. He quit painting, period, I think by 1990. I got together with him a few times to go trout fishing, and at one point he just said, 'I'm done.' He said, 'I'm a people person, and I'm tired of sitting in that studio every day painting by myself.' He said he felt like he was losing touch with reality."

Miller says that the last he heard, Scholer was working in the fly-fishing department at a Cabela's in Owatonna, in southeastern Minnesota.

"My wife says I overanalyze," Scot Storm says, and it's easy to believe as the amiable onetime North Dakota State University wrestler and former architect moves around the thousand-square-foot studio of his rural Freeport, Minnesota, home. He sets down his coffee cup and moves toward a painting on a far wall, a horizontal canvas showing more than a dozen pintail ducks in flight over a reedy marsh. He grabs a ruler and a straightedge and, gesturing at different places on the canvas, explains how he applies "the rule of thirds" to organizing the areas of darkness and light in his paintings, and how he triangulates a canvas to identify the painting's focal point.

"In this case I decided on pintails. I know the landscape is heavily weighted over here, and I wanted something to weight the painting here, so I wanted my main subject over here just in a preliminary sense. So I'll lay in a diagonal line like this on the top, and from that diagonal line I'll go up from the bottom corner and intersect it at a ninety-degree angle."

He concedes that his analytical approach to composition "may have been something I picked up in architecture. But I'm sure there are others that use it."

At this moment in April 2010, these rules of composition are the only aspects of his 2010 Federal Duck Stamp Contest entry about which he is certain. Having won the contest in 2003 with an entry featuring a pair of flying redheads, and having finished second in 2009 with a striking painting of swimming wood ducks, Storm finds himself, less than four months before the August deadline, with lingering doubts about which species he'll paint.

"I'm ninety-five percent sure it's Canada geese," he says. "But I'm vacillating between that and northern shovelers."

Storm understands the stakes as well as anyone. His previous win triggered an avalanche of interest in his work, making possible a move from his family's starter home in Sartell to their larger and more comfortable home in Freeport, "the city with a smile," whose 565 residents don't necessarily mind being a nearly two-hour drive from the urban center of Minneapolis. The Storms' new house sits on four acres and is an idyllic place for Scot and Kris to raise their twelve-year-old twins, as well as two Labrador retrievers and an ambitious Maltese named Brutus Maximus. Once confined to a work space measuring seven and a half by twelve feet and jammed with his painting desk, bookshelves, a formatting printer, and his computer, Storm now paints at a drafting table bathed in light from two windows, one of which overlooks a pond where he has built a blind from which he can photograph the waterfowl that use his property as a way station. The house also has enough garage space for three vehicles and a production and warehousing area where Scot makes his own prints and Kris still runs the business. Photos of all four family members in camouflage hunting clothes hang on a studio wall.

Storm already can feel his 95 percent certainty about the Canada geese eroding. He has lost confidence in his annual Duck Stamp Contest entry once before. Four days before the deadline for the 2003 contest, he abandoned the entry he'd been working on for months and started an entirely new one.

That was the entry that ended up winning it all. He is sure the geese would make a good painting. But he also knows that when you reduce a painting to the size of a duck stamp, it needs strong contrast and bright colors to stand out. The geese aren't quite what he needs.

But he's running out of time. Spring is when Storm usually focuses on commissioned paintings for clients and for Ducks Unlimited, which relies on wildlife art to raise money for conservation. He has a Plan B, the northern shovelers, but he isn't sure when he might be able to rethink his entry. And he isn't entirely ready to give up on those geese. Panic?

"I haven't yet."

As the deadline nears, the choice becomes clearer. He tries both paintings, then puts them away for a while. "When you look at the need for contrast and bright colors that you accentuate for state and federal designs . . . once I got the geese painted, they just didn't appeal to me as a duck stamp entry."

Among his many reference photos of flying shovelers, Storm finds shots that, when assembled into a composite image, seem more vibrant and better suited for a stamp design. "While you're painting a piece, and for a short period after, your mind gets blind to it because you see it so many times. You don't see things clearly. But I had a chance to put them away for a while and think about it, and in the end I decided to go with my gut feeling."

The painting of two shovelers that he enters not long before the contest deadline is a striking composition of two birds in flight. The drake in the foreground is a controlled kaleidoscope of blue, green, white, brown, and black. The hen behind it, about half as large, is a muted brown. They soar against a sky filled with pink and purple clouds, with a cattail-crowded lake and marsh below.

"I'm never completely happy with a painting," Storm says. "I'll have my doubts all the way up until the contest."

The only time he didn't have doubts, he says, was when his painting won.

## ROUND TWO

VETERANS OF THE Federal Duck Stamp Contest know
there's a different feel to the second day of judging, and
that's apparent as the faithful file into Berkeley's David Brower
Center for the second and third rounds of the 2010 contest. If
the start of Round One was all about the American dream—
about the delectable idea that anybody can win an art contest in
which the art is judged strictly on its merits, regardless of the
artist's name or reputation—then the start of Round Two is all
about facing the cold reality that some artists are simply more
skilled than others.

Round One is a champagne toast to giddy hope and bound-
less possibilities; Round Two is a bracing shot of whiskey before your Civil War surgeon gets to work with his saw.

Only 28 of the 235 competitors have survived the brutal "In"
or "Out" cull of the first round the day before. Neither the
judges nor most of the audience members know who painted
the chosen works, but among them are Mark Berger's flying
Canada geese, Sherrie Russell Meline's nesting Canada goose,
seaside brant by Missouri's Adam Nisbett and North Carolina's
Kip Richmond, swimming shovelers by Bruce Miller and

Gerald Mobley, Scot Storm's flying shovelers, Robert Steiner's swimming ruddy, Minnesotan Rebecca Latham's pair of swimming Canada geese, and the paintings submitted by fellow Minnesotans Michael Sieve and Jim and Bob Hautman—the only three first-round survivors who chose to paint those familiar birds of the Western flyway, specklebelly geese.

This assembly of judges—the one Duck Stamp Program chief Pat Fisher called "one of our most qualified judging panels ever"—seems particularly confident in its first-round assessments. Together, the five judges could have brought as many as twenty-five excluded paintings back into contention. But as Larry Mellinger, the Interior Department attorney, explains at the start of Round Two, only six pieces that were voted "Out" the day before have received an overnight reprieve. These are a floating ruddy by Phillip Crowe of Franklin, Tennessee; a nesting specklebelly by Thomas Bishop of Scottsdale, Arizona; a pair of flying Canada geese by John Brennan of Lutz, Florida; a pair of flying brant by Robert Van Hoose of Lake Village, Indiana; a placid pair of floating Canada geese by Shari Erickson of Beavercreek, Oregon; and the flying shovelers by South Dakota's Adam Grimm, the 1999 contest winner, whose painting sent a shocked murmur through the crowd when it received only two "In" votes in the first round. The inclusion of these six in the second round boosts the total number of survivors from twenty-eight to thirty-four. The thirty-four paintings await their second star turn in a box on the floor to the judges' right, arranged in order of their assigned number, from low to high, based on their date of receipt.

It may mean something; more likely it means absolutely nothing. But for those artists who annually parse previous contest results for clues about what choices might give them an edge in future contests, it's worth noting that exactly half of the paintings advancing to Round Two depict birds floating on water. Of the other seventeen paintings, nine depict birds in either a standing or a sitting position on terra firma, and eight show birds in the air. All but four of the survivors were painted by men.

A species breakdown of the chosen paintings reveals that nine depict what Bruce Miller calls "goofy-looking" shovelers, eight show blue-billed ruddy ducks, eight are of Canada geese, five depict brant, and, with the Round Two reprieve granted Bishop's nesting specklebelly, only four of the thirty-four first-round survivors depict that particular species.

To add a bit of official pomp to the proceedings in Berkeley, Dan Ashe, the deputy director of the U.S. Fish and Wildlife Service, has flown to the Bay Area the night before. In his dark suit, starched blue shirt, and gold necktie—apparently one of only two neckties at the gathering, the other worn by Jerome Ford, another ranking D.C.-based official from the service's Migratory Bird Program, who is introducing Ashe around—the deputy director stands out as a visiting delegate from Planet Washington, and one who clearly seems destined for bigger things.

Ashe's father was a career Fish and Wildlife employee who retired in 1990. Ashe earned a bachelor's degree in biological sciences from Florida State University and a graduate degree in marine affairs from the University of Washington. His master's thesis, on estuarine wetland mitigation, was published in the *Coastal Zone Management Journal* in 1982.

From 1982 until 1995, Ashe was a U.S. House of Representatives staff member for the former Committee on Merchant

Marine and Fisheries. During his thirteen-year stint on Capitol Hill, he advised the committee's members on a wide range of environmental policy issues, including endangered species and biodiversity conservation, ocean and coastal resources protection, the National Wildlife Refuge System, the National Marine Sanctuaries Program, the Clean Water Act, wetlands conservation, fisheries management and conservation, and offshore oil and gas development.

From 1998 to 2003, Ashe served as chief of the National Wildlife Refuge System, directing the operation and management of the system and its land acquisition program. During his tenure, the system grew at an unprecedented rate. He later was appointed science adviser to Fish and Wildlife, followed by his appointment as the service's deputy director for policy. While blessed with the good looks and disarming smoothness of a career politician, he's exactly the kind of articulate, experienced, and qualified public servant that, in a perfect world, would always rise to the top in government service.

But as he sips coffee in the Brower Center lobby before the start of the second round, the rangy, square-jawed Ashe drops the aura of rank and power and talks frankly about the critical nature of, and challenges facing, the Federal Duck Stamp Program.

"The threats we're facing, that we've always faced—habitat loss, fragmentation, water shortages, disease in wildlife—are all there, and all increasing because they're fundamentally related to human ecology," he says. "And there are going to be more human beings on the planet, so those traditional threats are going to get worse. We're learning more and more about climate change and the immediate near- and long-term effects related to that, so the need for the resources to support conservation is going to increase substantially."

Ashe leans forward to emphasize his point that the Duck Stamp Program is a model one that shows how a "user community"—hunters—can make a sustained and meaningful commitment to conservation: "We need it more than ever."

The federal official looks around the room filled with artists and wildlife art enthusiasts, perhaps recognizing the somewhat archaic nature of a contest dedicated to a pursuit that's been around for tens of thousands of years—brushing paint onto a surface. (And yes, contest regulations specify that entries must be hand-drawn—to emphasize this, organizers underscored and placed in quotes the word "<u>hand-drawn</u>" in the official rulebook.)[1]

"Do we need an actual stamp?" Ashe asks. "I guess the purely technical response to that is no. But I'm a waterfowler, have been since I was a young boy, and the duck stamp is an important tradition. There are lots of things in life that we don't need. But duck stamps enrich the tradition of waterfowl hunting. The artwork is like art in any context: It enriches our lives. And the collecting side of the duck stamp is an important institution and tradition in and of itself. Those are things that are extremely valuable, and the whole experience of waterfowling would be diminished if we didn't have the stamp. It certainly would be for me."

True, he says, it's possible now to buy an electronic duck stamp online. "We've tried to make it easier, and we've adapted our enforcement practices so that you don't have to have a physical stamp. I think we've taken advantage of the modern techniques of distribution and marketing to make it easier for people to acquire the stamp. And we certainly can do more in the future. That helps to support the stamp and the tradition overall."

And yet, Ashe says, the tradition of issuing a physical stamp has value at a time when the program is struggling with an ongoing and more formidable problem—getting the disparate constituencies of hunters and "nonconsumptive conservationists," including birders, to recognize the effectiveness of the Duck Stamp Program in achieving their shared goal of conserving wetlands and other wildlife habitat. He doesn't pretend to have the solution.

"I guess if I knew the answer to that question, we'd be in a much different place, maybe. But the key to that is education and communication. Having the competition in a place like this, and having our first-day-of-sale events in partnership with Bass Pro at one of its retail outlets, you're engaging a different dimension of even the sporting community. All of those are ways of reaching more people."

Ashe pauses before turning to the common thread that binds people not just in the Brower Center this morning, but everywhere on the planet. "We're all consumers," he says. "Getting people to realize that everything we do, every day, consumes wildlife. We now know, with climate change, when we adjust the thermostat on our air conditioner or heater, we're consuming habitat for the polar bear. And when we drive a vehicle, when we fly in an airplane, we're colliding with birds and other wildlife. We consume wildlife in our day-to-day activities."

He sweeps a long arm across the milling crowd. "Here's a segment of the population, hunters, who recognized a long time ago that we're consuming wildlife as a part of this passion that we share. We have to, first of all, realize that we're consumers, and then have the conviction to give back to that resource to ensure that it's sustained. And waterfowl, more so than any other category of wildlife, demonstrate that we can do that if we take care. We've sustained this commitment to conserving this habitat on which these creatures depend."

Not so with other species, even other birds, Ashe says. "The vast majority of other bird populations are in decline, because we haven't really been able to make that connection between day-to-day human activities that are driving the consumption of habitat. Certainly the duck stamp can provide us with a model, but the difficulties are that the pathways of consumption are less direct. It's harder to see that if you're sitting in an office building, that building is taking birds, or if you're driving across a bridge, then that bridge is contributing to bird mortality. It's a lot harder to link those individual activities to the need to conserve birds over a very broad scale."

Ashe describes the "magic" of the Duck Stamp Program in personal terms: "I'm a hunter in Maryland, but I know that the birds I'm hunting in Maryland are coming from a long way away, and that they depend on habitat between me and arctic Canada. So I'm willing to make that investment, to put money into the conservation of that habitat, as well as habitat in my home state. With other aspects of the consumption of wildlife, we haven't been able to make that kind of direct connection."

That same awareness of the migratory nature of birds—and that the responsibility for managing them does not stop at state lines or national borders—was the foundation of the original legislation that created the Duck Stamp Program. It continues to guide some of the public debate about conservation.

"You're seeing that now with species like sage grouse, which in the profession we call a 'resident species,' meaning that individuals in that species don't migrate," Ashe says. "But they occupy a range that crosses thirteen states in the West. And if we can't come up with a framework to protect them over thirteen states, then we're not going to be successful at conserving them. Especially as we confront issues like climate change, we're learning more and more that protecting individual places is probably not going to be sufficient to protect these populations that depend upon habitat across a broad expanse of the landscape. So we have to think at a larger scale and through longer periods of time."

How do you get birders to buy the same revenue stamp as the hunters they often loathe? The challenge, Ashe says, is to instill in bird-watchers the same sense of responsibility that hunters have demonstrated since 1934. The tricky part is convincing birders that they, too, are wildlife consumers.

"Even though the act of visually encountering a bird or capturing it photographically doesn't consume the bird itself, if the bird is not there, then [the birders'] activity can't take place. It's dependent on the presence of that animal. And so [birders] should make an investment in that, and it should become a part of the tradition of their endeavor. It should be a point of personal, individual, and collective responsibility within the birding community . . . If you're a birder, even if it's not a regulatory requirement, there should be some way to display a duck stamp, and that should be a point of social pressure within that community, so that if you're a responsible birder, then you would have a stamp, maybe on the lanyard of your binoculars. I think that's something that could be an important contribution in the future."

Ashe imagines a day when bird-watchers in the field will judge their fellow birders harshly if they don't see them displaying a duck stamp. "With waterfowlers, it's a requirement," he says. "But I've been hunting waterfowl since I was seventeen. My license has been checked in the field maybe twice that I can remember. If that requirement were repealed tomorrow, would waterfowlers continue to buy stamps? I would hope the majority would. But you certainly don't hear any clarion call from waterfowlers in opposition to the stamp, even as we're trying to get an increase in the stamp price."

His optimism is admirable. But even as he speaks, it's clear that the Duck Stamp Program will, once again, not be a high priority for the next Congress. The Great Recession is showing no signs of ending in the autumn of 2010, and polls are indicating that voters are preparing to vote out the Democratic majority that was swept into Congress with the election of President Barack Obama. The Tea Party, rallying around the less-government banner, is in undeniable ascent, and the only clarion echoing across the land at the moment sounds less like a call to arms to defend waterfowl habitat and more like demands for a reduction of the federal deficit and an extension of the George W. Bush–era tax cuts.

The Brower Center auditorium is slightly more crowded for Round Two than it was the day before, and there's a heightened sense of anticipation. Adding to the tension is the presence of Ashe and others from D.C. officialdom, and the quiet, unannounced arrival of a bit of duck stamp royalty.

Three-time winner Jim Hautman, wearing blue jeans and a casual black long-sleeve pullover, strolls into the Brower Center only a few minutes before the start of the second-round judging, along with wife Dorothy and another couple, friends from the area. Despite his low-key entrance, the spreading word that a Hautman is in the building creates a noticeable buzz. Hautman seems oblivious to it as he and his effervescent wife take seats with their friends in the back of the auditorium, about as far from the judging panel as possible. Brother Bob, whose painting also sailed into the second round with five "In" votes, is planning to watch the streaming video webcast on his computer back home in Delano, Minnesota.

Mellinger, the attorney, explains that judging in Round Two will follow the same basic format as in Round One, except that the "In" and "Out" placards have been replaced with placards bearing the numbers "1" through "5." The judges will assign each painting a point score, with one being the lowest and five being the highest. The lowest cumulative score a painting can receive in the second round is a five; the highest, a twenty-five.

In addition to a rigid set of basic requirements—all entries must measure ten inches wide and seven inches high, and be surrounded by arctic-white matting no more than a quarter inch thick—all competitors are encouraged to create their paintings with three things in mind: artistic impression, anatomical correctness, and suitability for reproduction on a stamp that will measure only one and three quarter inches long and one and a half inches wide. Mellinger explains that in this round the judges will focus even harder on these three filters.

In the critical realm of judging anatomical correctness, they'll have some help. As they have since the mid-1980s, the contest organizers have recruited a waterfowl biologist to assist the judges in determining if, for example, a bird's plumage is consistent with the foliage in the painting's background. Painting a duck with spring plumage against a background showing fall foliage would be inconsistent, and therefore problematic—the equivalent of painting Mona Lisa with a full beard, at least among those who know waterfowl. And since the fiasco of 1984, when the judges infamously chose a red-eyed wigeon with no primary flight feathers as the winner, the Duck Stamp Contest folks have been keenly aware of the need for anatomical accuracy.

The assigned biologist is somewhat of a phantom presence at the contest, the man behind the curtain. He's in the room with the judges before and between judging rounds, and by all accounts the judges seek his counsel with increasing intensity as they narrow the field. But since program chief Pat Fisher carefully restricts access to the consulting biologist before each contest, his role remains a bit mysterious.

From 2005 to 2009, longtime Fish and Wildlife biologist Ray Bentley of Blodgett, Oregon, served as the contest's waterfowl expert, counseling each year's judges about the physical and behavioral characteristics of the eligible species. Bentley offered a candid assessment of the consulting biologist's role in a 2009 e-mail to one artist who'd had the temerity to ask Bentley about the job, and that explanation helps open the curtain for a peek at the biologist behind it. In his e-mail, Bentley cataloged his attention to color, scale, anatomy, posture, and habitat and noted, "I am very careful not to impart my opinion to the judges, and in fact remain completely reactive to their questions during Round One voting."

By Round Three, when Bentley said the judges "are examining every detail of the entries *and* the artist's depiction of those details," he would "submit comments on the final entries, but focus *only* on technical parameters and only make statements suggesting inaccuracies that I feel would/could be detected by future observers and thus be questioned as appropriate as a winner." In general, he wrote, an artist's "strict adherence to realism, near perfection in technical parameters, [and] good composition for stamp purposes has produced entries that score high and end up as finalists."

Lending a note of tragedy to the 2010 contest, though, is Bentley's recent accidental death, which occurred just three months after the 2009 contest. The passionate fifty-two-year-old pilot, who frequently conducted aerial waterfowl surveys from a small single-engine plane, died along with another Fish and Wildlife biologist on January 17, 2010, when their plane crashed while the two men were surveying estuaries along the Oregon coast.[2] The contest's organizers honored Bentley with a memorial plaque during the annual first-day-of-sale ceremony, which took place in June at a Bass Pro store in Maryland.

"Ray often said he had two passions," the tribute read. "The first was wildlife, and the second was aviation. We would add a third—he was passionate about duck stamps, and he proved it time and time again during the contests. In fact, last year he made certain he would be conducting an aerial survey near the site of the Federal Duck Stamp Contest so that he could participate, not wanting any of his colleagues to get the job. We all admired and loved Ray, and we will sorely miss him."

Organizers tapped Thom Lewis, one of Fish and Wildlife's flyway biologists in training, to fill Bentley's role during the 2010 contest. But there has been no announcement of his presence, no introduction of Lewis to the audience. In fact, the biologist is spending a lot of time in the Brower Center's second-floor assembly room, where the judges received their pre-contest briefing and to which they will retreat during breaks between today's rounds. Fisher has promised them that "the green room is theirs alone and off-limits to everyone but a select few, myself, and our waterfowl expert." To say that Lewis is keeping a low profile during the proceedings would be a profound understatement.

Back onstage, Mellinger again discourages any audience oohing or aahing that might influence the judges. "We will take the five highest scores to go into the third and final round," he continues. "So there will be at least five paintings in the final round, maybe more."

Assistant Marie Strassburger hands Mellinger the first painting of Round Two, artist Adam Oswald's pair of floating ruddy ducks, and the attorney reverently presents it to Mike Chrisman, the nearest judge, before continuing down the line. After all five judges have given it a fresh look, Mellinger asks them to vote. The judges shuffle their placards, then each hold up a number between one and five that, in the final tally, will either help move the painting and its creator one step closer to artistic immortality or not.

3. 4. 3. 3. 3.

A sixteen out of a possible twenty-five—not a bad result for Oswald, but at this point there's no way to know whether it will be enough to advance the painting into the final round, or even get it included in the traveling tour of the 2010 contest's top point-getters. The judges have thirty-three more paintings to consider.

If Oswald's strong start has buoyed the other artists still in contention, it's a short-lived confidence booster. The next painting, Harold Roe's floating shoveler, manages only ten points. The third, Phillip Crowe's single floating ruddy, is greeted with a grim, glowing line of white placards reading 3, 2, 1, 1, 1— only eight total points out of the possible twenty-five. Two surviving paintings of Canada geese on the wing, one by Rod Lawrence and the other by Mark Berger, earn an identical fourteen points. For Berger, the supposedly missing flight feather isn't the issue; those prominent feet apparently are. While the painting itself is strong, judge Joe Garcia will later say that "the legs seemed a little heavy."

After a year of gathering research photography, soliciting design input from friends and fellow artists, and enduring relentless back pain as he created his piece, Berger is clearly stung by one judge's decision to give his piece only a single point.

"I'm out," he whispers.

The cull continues, but a clear leader emerges just three paintings later. Jim Hautman's pair of standing specklebellies makes its way down the line of judges. Upon the "Please vote" command, five white placards shoot into the air and trigger a restrained gasp from the crowd.

5. 5. 5. 5. 4.

Twenty-four points out of a possible twenty-five. Such a high score is hardly without precedent—in the final round of the 1998 contest, Jim Hautman's third and most recent win, his pair of flying greater scaup received all fives, a perfect score—but the judges' enthusiasm for certain works over others has become acutely apparent in Round Two. Jim Hautman's confidence that his piece is "as good an entry as I've had" does not seem misplaced.

Seven paintings later, another murmur ripples through the crowd after Bob Hautman's single standing specklebelly passes before the panel.

5. 5. 3. 5. 4.

The twenty-two points give Hautman the second-highest total of Round Two so far, behind only his brother Jim's.

Others' fates are quickly decided. The pair of flying shovelers by Adam Grimm, whose painting was brought back into Round Two after receiving only two "In" votes during the first round, receives a strong eighteen, as does Maryland's Charles Shauck's single floating ruddy. Rebecca Latham was the only member of Minnesota's painting Latham family—including mother Karen and sister Bonnie—to get beyond the first round. Her painting of swimming Canada geese gets seventeen points. So do Dee Dee Murry's standing, sun-kissed Canada goose and previous winner Gerald Mobley's pair of swimming shovelers. That's one point more than the judges award former winner Sherrie Russell Meline for her close-up image of a nesting Canada goose, which judge John Eadie later says he found nicely composed and appealing, but which other judges apparently found awkwardly posed and with too short a neck. The floating ruddy painted by fellow Californian Robert Steiner manages only fifteen points.

Previous winner Bruce Miller, who painted his swimming shoveler in less than four working days just before the deadline, lamented shortly before the start of the judging, "I wish I could have had more time to work on the background and probably smooth it out. I like the dynamics of the piece, but probably should have finished it better." The judges seem to agree; they give his shoveler only thirteen points. The pair of flying shovelers by previous winner and 2009 second-place finisher Scot Storm receives only thirteen points as well.

When the judges finish voting on the final painting of Round Two, many audience members set to work scanning their detailed do-it-yourself scoring sheets, which the organizers distributed the day before. The top five scores are twenty-four, twenty-two, eighteen, seventeen, and sixteen. Eleven artists achieved a score of sixteen or more, and their works will move into the third and final round.

The AV guy cues up some music for the short break before Round Three, and many in the crowd of artists, collectors, hunters, and conservationists filter into the lobby to parse the second-round results. In the dim recesses of the auditorium, high above the judging panel, top vote-getter Jim Hautman stays in his seat and allows himself a smile.

"I think they should stop right now," he says. "That went great. I can't believe it."

He shakes his head at the improbability that, at least so far, he and older brother Bob are the two favorites. "I can't believe that. I was really worried about that shoveler, Number 177"—he guesses correctly that it's by Gerald Mobley. "That's the one that had me worried. I don't know what it was about it, but coming in here, I thought that was the painting to beat."

Hautman thinks back to his struggle to find just the right backdrop for his pair of standing specklebellies. He ended up with a dramatic, gathering storm of dark gray clouds. The static-electric prickle of that background meshes dramatically well with the posture of the two geese, which seem to be on high alert for trouble. The painting conveys what many of the other entries are missing—an organic connection between the environment and the birds.

"The background, it plays such a key part, but you don't really want to notice it," Hautman says.

He isn't naïve enough to believe the contest is over. He's been through it often enough to know that Round Three can be a minefield of possibilities. At the moment, the judges are sequestered in the green room with Lewis, the biologist. They're giving each of the eleven final paintings an intensely close look, checking for anatomical or other inaccuracies, imagining how each might look when reduced to stamp size. Jim Hautman and everyone else at the Brower Center know that the best paintings don't always win. Still, Hautman manages another smile.

"I couldn't ask to be in a better position at this point. But I'll tell you what. If it isn't me, it's gonna have to be Bob. It's pretty exciting, I'll tell you. Talk about an adrenaline rush."

# WHAT IS ART, ANYWAY?

Almost every year for the past decade, one contestant has dutifully paid his $125 Federal Duck Stamp Contest entry fee knowing that his bird is likely to be stomped to death, unceremoniously, in the very first round. The odds against its getting even a single "In" vote have proved predictably staggering year after year, and even as he prepares to submit his swimming shoveler for the 2010 contest, he knows it is likely to go down in flames within minutes after the judging starts in Berkeley.

But make no mistake: Rob McBroom is no masochist. He's as thoughtful about his annual Duck Stamp Contest painting as any other competitor and can articulate his artistic choices and process better than most. Because he believes deeply in what he's doing, he approaches the contest each year with missionary zeal. Which is why his disqualification from the 2003 contest haunts him still, and why he's reconsidering the idea he has for his shoveler's bill as the August submission deadline approaches.

"I pushed the limits in 2003, and I paid for it," the thirty-six-year-old artist recalls, sitting in the living room of his home in

North Minneapolis, the neighborhood where he grew up. "My own hubris did that."

McBroom defies easy labels. He's an avant-garde artist who works part-time at the Minneapolis Institute of Arts and as the office manager for Amphetamine Reptile Records, occasionally signs his e-mails with double entendre pseudonyms ("Oliver Klozoff"), and already has owned two hearses in his short lifetime. His exposure to wildlife has, for the most part, involved road-flattened raccoons and a few opossums. Nearly four months before the August 15 deadline, he answers the door of his home— a home he shares with a dead-eyed gray cat named Shark and another, a former stray, named Susan—wearing a double-breasted green suit for which he paid a thrift store seven dollars, a white dress shirt, a yellow power tie, and what looks to be a large Pac-Man pin on the suit's lapel. Friends call him Noodles.

He is, in short, exactly the kind of artsy urban hipster who might take ironic glee in subverting the rigid Duck Stamp Contest rules and defying the judges' clear preference for natural, photorealistic wildlife art. And true, his paintings do stand out, adorned as they are with glitter, rhinestones, corporate and other logos, and, in 2001, a scorchingly filthy monologue from a porn movie translated into Morse code and disguised as rain falling on a black scoter.

But the 2003 fiasco wasn't the result of subversion, just an uncharacteristic lapse in his attention to detail. McBroom moves across the living room, looking for the offending work among his many ongoing projects, including a series of portraits of all the U.S. presidents in which he uses logos and other familiar images to create the presidents' facial features. (In one of the two paintings of Grover Cleveland, the president's nose and mustache are an inverted image of the face and antlers of Bullwinkle, the fabled cartoon moose. In the other—Cleveland gets two portraits, since he had two nonconsecutive terms—the president's mustache is the familiar Batman symbol, upside down.) When McBroom locates the 2003 Duck Stamp Contest painting, he angles it into the spring light from a nearby window.

"Here we go," he says. "See this cologne-sample card? It says 'Dune' in there. The 'Dune' is what got me disqualified, because it was embossed, and that fell under the 'No lettering' rule. So it was sent back ahead of time with a letter saying, 'Sorry, here's what you did.'"

The rebuke still stings. But now, seven contests later, McBroom remains subversive. Like Bruce Miller, Scot Storm, and fifty-nine other 2010 competitors, he has decided to paint the northern shoveler. Unlike the others, though, McBroom thinks it might be better to accentuate the duck's goofiness.

"Right off the bat, I knew I wanted to use the Shell oil logo for the bill," McBroom says of his in-progress painting of the bird floating on a placid pond. Just as quickly, though, he decided the Shell-logo bill wasn't sparkly enough. "I put a hologram sticker of Mount Rushmore on there, inside the shell. I found it at a surplus store here in town. Then I'll turn this part into glitter, and I'll put oval-shaped rhinestones right there."

He points out several other familiar logos within the painting, including one from the Camp Fire Girls. "The Batman logo is right there in the chest feathers," he says, earnestly noting that "the Batman symbol shows up quite often in my work."

But the hologram . . . that's where things really get murky. "The rules don't specifically say you can't use holograms, but there's rules like 'no scrollwork,' 'no lettering,' 'no photography.' They do allow some collage, and so I tend to go that way. Because what it really comes down to is: I didn't make that sticker; I'm just stealing it and cutting it up."

Now he's having second thoughts about that added sparkle. He sighs. "I might try to find a way to darken that a little."

What is art, anyway? That unanswerable question runs like a dark river just beneath the surface of any conversation about wildlife art, and Rob McBroom's quixotic quest to inject more rhinestones and glitter into the photorealistic world of pro-am competitive duck painting each year is as good a place as any to tap into it.

The world of high art—that is, the kind of art that ends up in museums and on the syllabi of college art-appreciation courses—often wrinkles its collective nose at the whole genre of wildlife art, as if sniffing something steamy and organic left by one of those golf-course-befouling Canada geese. Never mind that wildlife art is one of our species's oldest forms of visual expression, with roots tracing back at least thirty thousand years to the extraordinary paintings of lions, horses, bison, and other animals discovered in 1994 by cave explorer Jean-Marie Chauvet in France's Ardèche Valley—a series of images that a lead researcher of the cave drawings called "one of the great masterpieces of all time."[1] And never mind that a lot of people today like wildlife art well enough to pay exorbitant sums to collect it. There remains a presumption among many art lovers that wildlife painting is mere illustration, and therefore not infused with the same profound truths, beauty, and meaning as real "art."

That's more than the sniffy perception of high art's gatekeepers; it's a demonstrable reality. Back in the mid-1980s, Ronald Baenninger, a psychology professor at Temple University, surveyed images of paintings in major art-history texts and 1,674 paintings from seventeen major museums in Europe and North America, including the Louvre, the Prado, the Uffizi, the British Museum, the Metropolitan in New York, the Hermitage, and the national galleries in both London and Washington.[2] He noted that 64 percent of the works from ancient Egypt and Persia contained images of animals. But during the next twenty-five hundred years, animals began disappearing from Western art. Of the surveyed paintings from the period when the artists of ancient Greece and Rome were in full production, 37 percent contained animals. By the twentieth century, Baenninger found, animals appeared in only 15 percent of the paintings.

The researcher offered several explanations for the disappearance of wildlife from the Western world's leading art museums and texts, including the obvious fact that animals are less a factor in day-to-day human life now than back when centaurs and satyrs were key symbols in major religions, or even when milk trucks were pulled by horses and mail arrived via the Pony Express. We're evolving away from jungles and farms and production systems that rely on animal labor and into nations of app downloaders and latte sippers, where even cows, pigs, and chickens seem somewhat exotic. With the exception of our pets, most interactions with animals today involve cooking, plating, and eating them. Simply put, artists and everyone else in industrialized society are exposed to animals less often these days, and so naturally artists don't paint animals as often as they used to.

The Federal Duck Stamp story begins with Jay N. "Ding" Darling, an editorial cartoonist and passionate conservationist, who became head of the Bureau of Biological Survey, which became the U.S. Fish and Wildlife Service. (Courtesy of the Jay N. "Ding" Darling Wildlife Society)

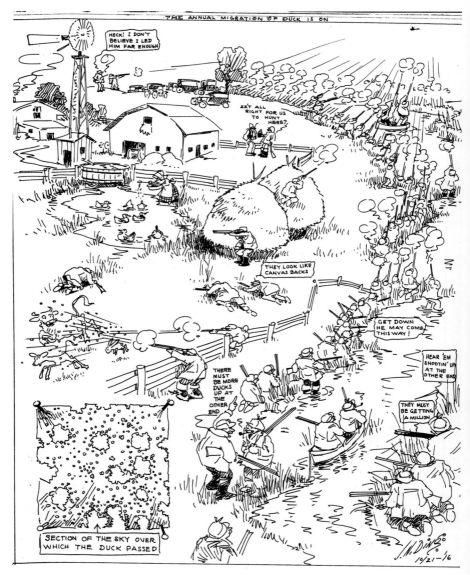

"The Annual Migration of Duck Is On" cartoon by Ding Darling, penned in 1916, helped make waterfowl conservation part of the national debate. (Courtesy of the Jay N. "Ding" Darling Wildlife Society)

A bird's-eye view of Minnesota's Prairie Pothole Region, considered the "duck factory" of North America. (U.S. Fish and Wildlife Service)

Minnesota's Thomas "Tuck" Hautman expressed his passion for waterfowl in paintings. His love of hunting helped inspire a modern dynasty. (Courtesy of Joe Hautman)

Going into the 2010 contest, brothers Joe, Bob, and Jim Hautman had held the title Federal Duck Stamp Artist nine times since 1989. (Courtesy of Joe Hautman)

The Hautman brothers also trace their wildlife art to their mother, Elaine, whose works—now hanging in Joe's home—include paintings in the style of those on the walls of France's Chauvet cave from thirty thousand years ago. (Photograph by Martin J. Smith)

Former winner Sherrie Russell Meline of Mount Shasta, California, begins her 2010 entry of a Canada goose by sketching in the image's major components. (Courtesy of Sherrie Russell Meline)

Meline's finished painting. She first entered the contest in 1985, drawn by the chance of big money: "They used to call it the million-dollar duck. That's changed immensely, but that's the way it was." (Courtesy of Sherrie Russell Meline)

Bruce Miller, the 1992 contest winner and a fan of Russian impressionism, enters a single northern shoveler for the 2010 contest. One judge deems it "a little painterly." (Courtesy of Bruce Miller)

Adam Grimm, the 1999 winner, composes his 2010 entry of flying shovelers in Photoshop using many photographs, then he paints the scene as realistically as possible. (Courtesy of Adam Grimm)

Artists guess what might appeal, or not, to the year's five unannounced judges. Mark Berger scrutinizes his Canada goose's webbed feet, which some judges consider a less attractive aspect of the bird. (Photograph by Martin J. Smith)

California artist Mark Berger's 2010 painting of Canada geese in flight does well, but one judge scores it lower than others because the legs of the lead goose "seemed a little heavy." (Courtesy of Mark Berger)

Scot Storm won the contest in 2003 and finished second in 2009. His 2010 entry of two flying shovelers acknowledges the judges' preference for photorealistic birds in natural settings. (Courtesy of Scot Storm)

Rob McBroom's predictably doomed 2010 painting features shovelers with rhinestones, corporate logos, and at least one possibly illegal hologram. (Courtesy of Rob McBroom)

Minneapolis artist Rob McBroom enters his provocative paintings to bridge the gap between avant-garde and wildlife art. His exposure to actual wildlife is limited to road-flattened raccoons and an occasional backyard opossum. (Photograph by Martin J. Smith)

Duck stamp collector William Webster first proposed that contest judging be made public. The 1966 decision to do so was the first step in the contest's transformation into the "*American Idol* for wildlife artists." (Photograph by Martin J. Smith)

Panel of contest judges voting during the first round in Berkeley, California. It was a slickly staged affair, even if the judging was merciless. (Photograph by Martin J. Smith)

California Audubon members at the 2010 Federal Duck Stamp Contest.
(Photograph by Martin J. Smith)

Decoy carving demonstration at the Federal Duck Stamp Contest in Berkeley.
(Photograph by Martin J. Smith)

Bob Hautman begins his 2010 entry with a pencil sketch of a single speckTebelly goose, chosen from the list of five eligible species that year. (Courtesy of Robert Hautman)

Early painting of Bob Hautman's specklebelly goose entry. Because the goose is a western bird, and correctly assuming the Berkeley judges would be from the West, both Bob and Jim Hautman opt to paint specklebellies. (Courtesy of Robert Hautman)

In addition to choosing a western flyway bird, Bob Hautman hopes to increase his chances with the judges by setting his specklebelly in a western landscape. (Courtesy of Robert Hautman)

Bob Hautman's final painting shows his goose against the backdrop of central California's Sutter Buttes. He also obscures the bird's feet to minimize its less attractive qualities. (Courtesy of Robert Hautman)

Three-time winner Jim Hautman translates his palm-sized study of specklebelly geese onto a regulation-sized surface, then refines it into a nearly finished painting, including orange clouds. (Courtesy of Jim Hautman)

The early version is exactly as Jim Hautman imagined it, including those carefully obscured feet, but he says something about it feels wrong. (Courtesy of Jim Hautman)

Jim Hautman tries to add some drama to the background clouds, but feels it still isn't working. (Courtesy of Jim Hautman)

Frustrated, Jim paints the background a flat gray, intending to start over. The whole time, he says, "the birds just sort of sat there." But then he realizes how well the gray makes the geese pop off the painting's surface. (Courtesy of Jim Hautman)

By the time Jim Hautman finishes, he feels confident about the painting. For the full eight-photo progression sequence of this painting, visit www.wildduckchase .com. (Courtesy of Jim Hautman)

"In one sense, the disappearance of animals from paintings came as a surprise to me, because a great many ordinary people in the United States like to look at pictures of animals," Baenninger wrote in 1987 in a journal called *Anthrozoös*, which is focused on the interactions of people and animals. "Stores in shopping malls that sell mass-produced things to hang on home walls always sell many paintings, photographs, and sketches of animals. There is a distinct genre of wildlife art that is very popular among large segments of the American public, particularly hunters and nature enthusiasts."

And yet, he wrote, "such wildlife art is virtually never exhibited in museums or galleries that show 'serious' art, and is largely ignored by the museum curators and art critics who shape the fashions and distribute the prizes in the art world."

Another reason, Baenninger suggested, might be that the very popularity of wildlife art gives it the taint of the masses, and therefore makes it seem unworthy of consideration by the discriminating guardians of high art. "The world of serious painting, like the world of serious music, may view general popularity with a certain amount of suspicion and even contempt," he wrote. "Modern tastemakers of the art world usually relegate art that is popular to the galleries of ordinary folk—calendars, greeting cards, and the walls of family rooms and dens where people spend most of their time at home. That is where most pictures of animals now are found. Just as popular music is generally not played by symphony orchestras in concert halls, popular art is seldom found hanging in museums and galleries."

Even some in the wildlife-art world see a clear distinction between high art and what ends up, for example, on the Federal Duck Stamp. In 1990, a writer for *Audubon* magazine[3] asked Russell A. Fink, an art dealer and the coauthor of a comprehensive, loose-leaf chronicle of Federal Duck Stamp Artists called *Duck Stamp Prints*, whether duck stamps even represented the finest in wildlife art, much less high art. Fink laughed.

"You're talking two different things," he said. "You want to talk art or do you want to talk duck stamps? This is a design contest; it's not an art contest. That's why the commercial artists are all winning it. They leave enough blank area to put the denomination . . . 'Void after . . . U.S. Department of the Interior . . .'"

In the same magazine piece, DeCourcy L. Taylor Jr., a wildlife artist and a past judge of a similar Ducks Unlimited contest inspired by the federal contest, told writer Ted Williams, "If you want to make money in art, you look for what appeals to the masses. And what appeals to the masses is rather hokey calendar art." He described most federal winners as "sappy illustrations because that's what appeals to the average consumer, who has the mentality of a twelve-year-old. Why are the best-rated TV shows what they are?"

An Illinois dealer, Burnett Harshman, singled out the 1983 winner—which appeared on the Duck Stamp Program's fiftieth-anniversary stamp in 1984–1985 and is one of the most popular designs on record—as a prime example of what can happen when the definition of art is left to a panel of five judges, who that year chose as the winner a painting of two swimming American wigeon with missing primary flight feathers. Those critical feathers had to be painted in after the contest was over, lest that embarrassing inaccuracy end up on the stamp itself.

"It's just terrible art," Harshman told Williams, referring to the flawed duck stamp image painted by William Morris, who at the time of his win had been painting for only two years, and who some believe created his painting based on a photo of a captive duck. "I don't blame that on Bill Morris; I blame that on the judging. If you went to the contest and watched them pick a painting [of a duck] that had no primary feathers and could not fly, you would have been sick. It also had a red eye; and I've never seen a red-eyed wigeon. They went through their great process of selecting, and they picked a red-eyed wigeon without any primaries as the design for the fiftieth-anniversary program. It was an absolute tragedy."

Added Bubba Wood, a Texas dealer, "The only guy who confuses duck stamps with art is the guy who wins the contest."

Not surprisingly, many duck painters and others disagree.

"It's a false argument," says three-time Federal Duck Stamp Contest winner Jim Hautman, upon whose studio mantelpiece in Chaska, Minnesota, sit two of his own impressionistic paintings—a landscape and a figurative portrait of a bearded old man. "I like all types of art. There's completely abstract stuff that I like, and I've done a lot of completely abstract stuff, too. There's people who even say that painting anything realistic is . . ."

He pauses. While all three Hautman brothers are quietly but fiercely competitive, they exhibit the calm of men who have nothing to prove. "I mean, there's every opinion in there. To say that subject matter has anything to do with whether something's art or not seems ridiculous . . . A nude is art, but a duck isn't art? I don't even think about it anymore."

Rebecca Latham, a young artist from Hastings, Minnesota, who along with her sister, Bonnie, followed their mother Karen's lead into the world of wildlife art, started out painting what she calls "splashy" floral watercolors. She soon got bored: "With realistic wildlife art, I have to know what I'm doing, and it has to be accurate, and that became more interesting to me."

To those who disparage realistic wildlife art in favor of, say, abstract art, Latham poses a variation of the exasperated question posed by Jim Hautman: "If you simplify something into just a shape, it would be art? But then if you turn it into something recognizable, it's not art?"

Bruce Miller, the 1992 Federal Duck Stamp Contest winner, has pushed his nature art away from realism in recent years, but he continues to compete in the contest. "That's the funny part about it. Critics have never accepted wildlife art as fine art. Which is a crock. I'll actually do a landscape painting as a release after doing a major wildlife painting, because a wildlife painting is a helluva lot harder than doing a landscape painting, which is considered fine art . . . In my world, wildlife art is just harder to do. A tree can look like any tree, but a chicken has to look like a chicken, and an elk has to look like an elk. I'm a perfect example of a person who does both, and who knows the stigma about wildlife art really is not fair."

David Allen Sibley of Concord, Massachusetts, the forty-nine-year-old author and illustrator of the enormously popular birding field guides that bear his name, recalls taking art classes as a young man at the community center in the Connecticut town where he grew up. "I remember one once-a-week evening class in particular that was taught by a professional artist, and he was constantly trying to get me to draw and paint something other than birds. The gist of it was, 'That's not art.' He wanted me to do what he considered 'real' art. The kinds of things I was doing in bird painting did not meet his definition of art. Just categorically, there was no way I could paint a bird and produce art."

Sibley cites the case of the late Robert Verity Clem, a Cape Cod artist who illustrated the classic 1967 book *The Shorebirds of North America*. Sibley admires Clem's work, which some have compared to that of Andrew Wyeth. Clem's watercolors for the book were immediately hailed as masterpieces of natural-history art.

"He was absolutely one of the best ever painters of birds," Sibley says. "I didn't know him well, but I saw him a few times over the last ten years. He did these spectacular paintings of shorebirds and quite a few other birds in the 1960s, but then he stopped and started painting landscapes, usually with birds in them. And the landscapes were gorgeous, and he was usually able to sell them to the small group of collectors who would buy any-thing he painted. But he would always say that he quit painting birds because he didn't get any respect for it. He had to paint landscapes to be taken seriously as an artist. He was very up-front and cynical about that."

Adam Grimm, the 1999 Duck Stamp Contest winner, offers a story strikingly similar to Sibley's art class tale, and embedded in that account of his journey from obscurity to duck stamp fame is a chapter that vividly demonstrates the divide between the worlds of high art and wildlife art.

On November 4, 1999, Grimm's painting of a mottled duck flapping its wings on the water was chosen as the design for the 2000–2001 Millennium Federal Duck Stamp, making him, at twenty-one, the youngest-ever winner of the federal contest. At the time, the Ohio native had been studying fine art at the Columbus College of Art and Design for a little more than two years. He'd been awarded a substantial scholarship, he says, and he did well in his classes and was on the school's equivalent of a dean's list. But the day he was notified of his win, he left school and drove home to his parents' house in Elyria, about two and a half hours north. He never went back to school.

"I was very unhappy at art school," recalls Grimm. "I actually had it out with a number of professors at the school, because it was like they were living in a bubble. I was going into the fine arts major because I wanted to do fine art. I wasn't really looking to do illustrations for a book or magazines or things like that. I wanted to do artwork that was of museum quality, except of wildlife."

His teachers gave him good grades, he says, because of his prodigious skills in everything from human-figure drawing to calligraphy to perspective work. "But my goal was not to do large abstracts; I was doing realistic-type work . . . It was nice paintings of ducks. And they had a serious problem with that."

Since he had been selling his art for years at art shows before he ever enrolled in art school, he felt he had a good feel for the marketplace. "This is the kind of stuff people want to buy," he says of wildlife art. He describes one of the episodes from his time at art school that was pivotal in shaping his views about the apparent divide between high art and wildlife art. He brought his third Duck Stamp Contest entry—which he'd developed during a Montana workshop led by former federal winners Daniel Smith and Bruce Miller, and which would eventually become the millennium stamp—into school to show it to a few professors whose work he respected. He caught one of them in the middle of a conversation with another professor who Grimm knew had a pronounced distaste for realistic nature art. When that professor offered that the painting "doesn't speak to me," Grimm asked him what he'd recommend.

"He said, 'It's just a duck. Maybe you could do something interesting.'" As an example, the teacher recommended painting a bulletproof vest onto the duck, as an oh-so-ironic statement about hunting. "And I'm just thinking, 'That's just so weird . . .'"

David Allen Sibley laughs after hearing an abbreviated version of Grimm's story. "I don't know what the relative numbers would be of people who actually make a living doing wildlife art compared to the people who actually make a living doing fine art, because I get the feeling the general public enjoys wildlife art more than fine art," he says. "Maybe it's just the people I hang out with. But [among] the people I know who have graduated with fine art degrees, it's a common point of view: If you're successful, that means you're not doing art anymore."

Applying that standard, John James Audubon today might be considered a hack. Sibley describes as "absurd" efforts to draw a distinction between Audubon's work, "which people are happy to hang in galleries and sell for very high prices and hang in the biggest art museums," and what today's bird artists do. "What Audubon was doing almost two hundred years ago was scientific illustration—taking birds and painting them as realistically as he could, and making nice compositions and telling a little story in each painting. He was driven by the same things that drive any of us to illustrate birds, so it's funny that *his* work is now considered art."

Deep down in the duck stamp Wonderland are a group of people who regard the annual contest and the resulting stamps as very serious art—and sometimes serious business. They're duck stamp collectors, and they're no less interesting a breed than the artists themselves. Bob Hautman recalls listening with unbridled curiosity as his brother Jim described the undiscovered world of collectors that he'd encountered after his first win, in 1989. "Oh geez," Bob says. "Jim would tell me about how he'd go to these stamp shows to sign stamps, and you'd see these collectors—"

He stands up and flips an imaginary binocular head-mounted magnifier down for up-close stamp viewing. "They're walking around, and they've got these OptiVisor[4] magnifying things on their heads, and these tweezers, and their little tools for picking up stamps, and they're like, you know . . . It's this whole new world I never knew about."

There's no shortage of evidence that stamp collectors tend to be older. And at a time when the U.S. Postal Service itself is suffering staggering financial losses as more and more mail traffic moves to the Internet,[5] the hobby of stamp collecting—which began in the mid-nineteenth century and was dubbed *philatélie* by a Frenchman in 1864—is on the wane. This, too, worries those who cherish the Federal Duck Stamp Program.

But if the migratory habits of ducks drive the need to preserve wetlands, then for decades duck stamp collectors have driven the aftermarket for practically everything else associated with the program. Duck stamps are, to collectors, much more than simply an official adornment for a hunting license or a contribution to the cause of conservation. Duck stamps are the longest-running series of stamps ever issued by the U.S. government, and the stamps represent a rare and fascinating unbroken chain of annual issues, little pieces of living folklore left like a paper trail back to one of the most dramatic periods of American history.

The best-known duck stamp collector is Jeanette Cantrell Rudy of Tennessee, a genteel Southern renaissance woman who numbers among her accomplishments a storied career in nursing, as well as victories in the Tennessee State Ladies Trap Championship in 1961, 1962, 1964, 1967, 1968, 1969, 1973, and 1975 and in the Tennessee Ladies Skeet Championship in 1968. She began collecting duck stamps in the 1960s, a hobby eventually underwritten by proceeds from her husband's burgeoning sausage business. During the decades that followed, she assembled what many consider the finest and most complete duck stamp collection in the world.

Clearly, no one fell deeper into the rabbit hole.

Rudy's collection includes the holy grail of the duck stamp world—the very first stamp ever sold. It features the drawing *Mallards Dropping In*, which former editorial cartoonist and Duck Stamp Program creator Ding Darling sketched on a shirt cardboard in 1934 and handed off as one of several possibilities to the U.S. Bureau of Engraving and Printing, which mistakenly assumed they were finished drawings, chose one, and began production on the first run of stamps. While upset that the historic first stamp did not represent his best work, Darling nonetheless was eager to get the program off to a strong start. On August 22, 1934, he participated in the ceremonial first sale of the stamp—a tradition that continues in the program's annual first-day-of-sale ceremony.

Darling autographed the "first" stamp and presented it to William Mooney, postmaster at the main post office in Washington,

D.C., making Mooney the world's very first duck stamp collector. Mooney affixed his stamp not to a hunting license but to Form 3333, a light blue card to be used by those who bought stamps but did not have hunting licenses. Mooney's form and the stamp on it—authentication papers soberly note a small rust mark left by a paper clip—later were bought by Texas stamp dealer Bob Dumaine, coauthor of the book *The Duck Stamp Story* and founder, in 1992, of the National Duck Stamp Collectors Society.

In 1989, Dumaine sold them to Rudy during a closed auction attended by the world's seven leading duck stamp collectors. She paid Dumaine $275,000 for them.

Her collection also includes a stunning variety of duck stamp curiosities, including stamps with the kind of mistakes in perforation and other printing anomalies that can make a collector's heart beat faster. But the gracious Rudy eventually stopped exhibiting her collection at many stamp shows after overhearing exhibitors at a booth beside hers saying they might as well go home, since their collections paled in comparison to Rudy's. That bothered her, and she claims she never exhibited at those smaller shows again. "Why should I negate anyone else's thrill and enthusiasm in it just because I want to be a hot shot?"[6]

In the early 1990s, Rudy started thinking about her legacy. She decided to loan parts of her collection and donate five hundred thousand dollars to the Smithsonian's National Postal Museum, which in 1996 opened the Jeanette Cantrell Rudy Gallery to host an exhibit titled Artistic License: The Duck Stamp Story.[7]

"You know, God's been good to me, and we all think about

our legacy," she once told an interviewer. "This would be something I leave for someone else. That's what a legacy is. And I've done this and enjoyed it so much. I hate to brag on it, but it *is* a fabulous collection. And I know that it is. Not that I'm anything special [but] I thought, 'Well everyone wants to be remembered somehow.' And [as] people without children, what are we going to do? We must find our way in the miles of life that we travel, before the end comes."[8]

One of Rudy's notable contemporaries in the world of duck stamp collecting is William Webster, who lives along Lake Pepin in Frontenac, Minnesota. Sitting in his home office, which feels like a tableau from a different era, Webster, still a vital and passionate man at eighty-four, recounts tales from more than six decades of duck stamp lore amid the *tick-tick-ticking* of the mechanical clock that serves as the soundtrack of a work space he shares with a secretary who has been with him for thirty-nine years.

A fan of wildlife art for as long as he can remember, Webster still counts among his most powerful childhood memories a personal encounter with the man himself, Ding Darling. Webster's parents often wintered on Florida's Captiva Island, as did Darling, and Webster once petitioned his father to ask the Pulitzer Prize–winning cartoonist for an original drawing of a duck. Not only did Darling oblige, but he inscribed it "To Billy Webster, Good Hunting."

A collector was born.

Webster bought his first duck stamp a few years later, in 1940, and by 1966 was so passionate about his hobby that he wrote a letter to artist Robert Hines, the 1945 contest winner, who had

later been hired to administer the Duck Stamp Program, a post
he would hold for thirty-two years.[9] "I asked if I could attend
the judging," Webster says.

That simple request proved to be a pivotal moment in the
evolution of the Federal Duck Stamp Contest. A few days before the judging for the 1967–1968 stamp design was to begin,
Webster received a reply from Hines telling him he was welcome to watch the judging process. "That was the first time
they let the public have access to it," he says. "It was just the five
judges and me."

Webster eventually helped convince federal officials to open
the event to a wider audience, and for the next thirty-three years,
without fail, he attended every judging. There's unmistakable
pride in his voice when he says that he has met all but four of
the Federal Duck Stamp Artists. He also was later instrumental
in convincing Ducks Unlimited to auction limited-edition
wildlife prints as a key component in its annual fund-raising
efforts. And these days, he'll proudly show off a collection that
includes not only one of the world's most complete sequences
of Federal Duck Stamps, much of which he keeps in a safe-
deposit box at a nearby bank, but also items such as hand-carved
decoys, decades-old correspondence with various duck stamp
personalities and dealers, and even the hunting log that a friend
of his father started in 1922.

At a certain point, Webster turned his passion for duck
stamps into a business opportunity that may have helped further blur the line between high and low art. In 1968, when
he was still a manufacturer's rep for the company Master Lock,
he founded a business in his garage and named it Wild Wings.
In 1970, Wild Wings began publishing signed and numbered

limited-edition prints of Federal Duck Stamp Contest winners and other wildlife art. The company launched a direct mail catalog touting its wares the year after that, and today it remains one of the leading publishers and distributors of wildlife, sporting, and nostalgic Americana art prints and art-related products.

At one point, Webster says, Wild Wings boasted a chain of twenty-two galleries around the country, 130 employees, and annual sales of $75 million, although those numbers represent a peak seen now only in the company's rearview mirror. Webster sold Wild Wings to giant outdoor retailer Cabela's in 2002 and these days serves only as an adviser to the acquired company, which is based in Lake City, Minnesota, about ten miles down Highway 61 from his Frontenac home. Among the touted products in its summer 2010 catalog are a $15.95 dual-light-switch cover bordered by hand-painted, cold-cast antler segments, a $19.95 "Carved Mallard & Loon Snack Dish," and $99.95 wood toilet seats featuring licensed animal paintings, including one of three noble-looking Labrador retrievers by 2003 Federal Duck Stamp Contest winner Scot Storm.

You might expect Rob McBroom, the reigning provocateur of the Federal Duck Stamp Contest and the lone avant-garde presence in this refuge of realism, to have a snarky, ironic take on the place that wildlife painting occupies, or doesn't, in the world of high art. But actually, he, too, has little patience with those who draw bright lines between art's various realms.

"I'm the first to admit that I think serious art doesn't have to be serious," he says as he's putting the finishing touches on his dangerously hologrammed shoveler for the 2010 contest. "Truth be told, there's a lot of contemporary art that I find just over-blown and boring. I'm not sure how many different meanings an all-white canvas can have, but damn if artists don't trot out new theories regularly."

Like Adam Grimm and David Allen Sibley, McBroom has concluded that "there's a lot of BS in art, and the artists either know it or are totally up their own asses about the importance of what they do."

He takes his annual Duck Stamp Contest submission seri-ously, but is under no illusions about the impact his efforts might have in bridging the gap between avant-garde art and wildlife art. A painting can only do so much, a lesson McBroom says he has learned while working in art museums, including the Walker Art Center from 1998 to 2004 and the Minneapolis In-stitute of Arts since 2006. "I can tell you that, even if something is considered a masterpiece, people spend virtually no time looking at art. I'd see patrons come in all the time and go, 'Van Gogh—check! Monet—check! We've been here forty-five sec-onds; let's find the Rembrandt!' I've seen some published studies of what the average time is for someone to spend with an art-work. Including the time spent reading the didactics, the mean time is barely over twenty-seven seconds, and the median time is seventeen seconds. That's none too impressive."

One of the reasons he loads up his Duck Stamp Contest en-tries with what he calls "razzle-dazzle" is to simply get people to interact somehow with his painting. McBroom calls it his "Benihana approach," in which audience members are drawn in by some initial showiness and realize later that they've actu-ally had a decent meal. "Artistically speaking, I prefer that over somebody overpromising a gourmet meal of soulfulness that turns out to be the equivalent of wet fish sticks on a Styrofoam plate.

"I know some art aficionados think you shouldn't have to cater to that element, and that it's superficially demeaning to 'real' art," he continues. "My take on it is, get the audience to look in the first place and hope they'll be interested enough to think about the piece instead of shoving pseudo-intellectual angst down their throats and then complaining that the Philistines don't get you."

More traditional wildlife artists, on the other hand, struggle with precisely the opposite problem. "The [perception] is it's all visual aesthetics and devoid of any content beyond that," he says. "That's why you haven't really seen any major active collecting [of wildlife art] by art museums. It falls to private enthusiasts."

For McBroom, small victories matter. He remembers fondly the glorious moment in 2008, when the judging for the 2009–2010 stamp was staged at the big art center in Bloomington, just south of Minneapolis. It was the moment when, for the first and only time to date, one of the five judges gave his painting an "In" vote during the first round. It was a futile gesture by a good-humored judge; the piece would have needed three "In" votes to move into the second round, and there was no real risk of McBroom's glittery, logo-filled profile of a long-tailed duck in winter plumage getting two more. (It's hard to say whether any of the judges noticed McBroom's sly circumvention of the rule forbidding artists to sign their painting, which he achieved by rendering the duck's cheek patch as a burnt umber thumbprint.) "I will say this," McBroom says. "When I watched my 2008 entry get that one vote, and the whole audience start

murmuring in disbelief—man, it's those little things that make
entering it each year worth it."

The Duck Stamp Program's Pat Fisher says she looks forward
to seeing McBroom's annual entry. Hearing that bit of news
makes McBroom smile.

"I'm fully aware that what I'm peddling has little chance of
even getting close to winning the Duck Stamp Contest," he says.
"But in entering each year, I hope that I'm making at least some
of the wildlife-art crowd see that there are different possibilities,
and making those who aren't into that stuff aware of a very good
conservation program. The Hautmans and the other ninety-nine
percent of the entrants are very good at what they do, but that
fan base is already established. The people who are into what I do
are a totally different crowd, so I'm trying to bring them into the
mix with the duck stamp traditionalists."

His intent, he says, "was never to be a jerk about making them
the way I do. And for the most part, the wildlife artists that I've
encountered have been really cool about it, with an exception or
two, once they realize I'm not doing it as a big middle finger to
them. Artists should be true to who they are as people when they
make work, and there's a real Minnesota-ness about the contest
that must be culturally ingrained within me, because I'm legiti-
mately interested in this as subject matter."

Do all the competitors really get McBroom? Actually, no.
Griped one New Jersey wildlife artist on an Internet message
board, "We call that guy 'The Sequin Guy' because he glues
sequins and buttons and glitter to his entry. He pays $125 every
year [and] follows none of the rules. He uses famous logos in his
pieces, which is another violation. And when he loses (he generally gets no score whatsoever) he rants on his website about

how he should have won. The only reason they accept his entry is because they think it's funny and it's one of their favorite moments to open it and see what's in store."[10]

Such is the fate of the daring and misunderstood. In the end, though, McBroom has no regrets about his decision to pony up the annual entry fee and spend countless hours working on a doomed painting. "That entry fee goes right back into keeping a program going that I think should be around, even if I weren't a part of it."

# ROUND THREE

ONLY ELEVEN ARTISTS have survived the carnage of the first two rounds of judging. Five of them are previous winners of the Federal Duck Stamp Contest, and all of them are professional wildlife artists, suggesting that even though the judges have no idea which artist painted which piece, America's duck-painting elite have risen to the top.

The five previous winners among the final eleven are California's Sherrie Russell Meline, Oklahoma's Gerald Mobley, South Dakota's Adam Grimm, and, of course, Minnesota's Jim and Bob Hautman. All of them are full-time professional wildlife artists. But then, so are the rest of the contenders: Washington's Dee Dee Murry, Maryland's Charles Shauck, Minnesota's Rebecca Latham, South Dakota's Russ Duerksen and Adam Oswald, and North Carolina's Kip Richmond.

During a break between the second and final rounds, the handicappers and some of the assembled artists study their scoring sheets as if they're racing forms. They're looking for clues about the judges' preferences, hoping against all logic that those clues might help them unlock the mystery for future contests, which of course will be refereed by an entirely different panel

of judges. So for them, here's a catalog of tantalizing—if sometimes contradictory and inconclusive—facts:

- Intentionally or not, the judges have been quite egali-
  tarian toward 2010's eligible species. All five are represented among the eleven finalists, with three paintings
  of ruddy ducks, three of Canada geese, two of northern
  shovelers, one of a brant, and two of specklebelly geese.
- The judges have shown an equal preference for paintings that depict birds on the water and those featuring
  birds on solid ground. Five paintings show birds on the
  water. Five others show birds standing or sitting on
  terra firma. Only one depicts birds in the air.
- Nothing in the judges' choices of finalists settles the debate about what many artists see as a clear trend toward
  simple backgrounds following the previous year's win by
  Maryland's Robert Bealle, whose painting of a floating
  American wigeon included nothing more than a bit of
  water in the foreground, a couple of reeds, and what
  could have been a creeping, dun-colored fog in the background. Five of the 2010 finalists fall into that simple-
  is-better school, but the remaining six include significant
  or even elaborate backgrounds and landscapes.
- Male dominance in the world of competitive duck painting remains an indisputable reality. However, it's worth
  noting that three of the eleven finalists are women, including former winner Sherrie Russell Meline.
- More than half of the eleven finalists come from two
  Prairie Pothole Region states, Minnesota and South
  Dakota. Still, the geographic spread of the other finalists

is remarkable: North Carolina, Washington, California, Oklahoma, and Maryland.

At high noon, the judges return from their secret second-floor lair and assemble again at the front of the auditorium, which is as crowded as it has been at any point during the two days of judging. This is The Show, the final round. Within an hour, all the speculation, handicapping, and guesswork will be done. Within an hour, America will have a new Federal Duck Stamp Artist.

Jerome Ford strides to the podium. One of the few African American faces in the room, the deputy assistant director of the U.S. Fish and Wildlife Service's Migratory Bird Program is a gregarious presence. He begins the final round by asking the three Duck Stamp Program staffers, "those ladies"—Pat Fisher, Elizabeth Jackson, and Laurie Shaffer—to stand for a round of applause. "I know this all goes rather quickly here, but this is a year-round process for them," he says. "Right after this contest, they're going to start preparing for next year's contest."

And with that, Ford reintroduces attorney Larry Mellinger, who explains that in this, the third round, the judges will be shown each of the eleven paintings that made it through the previous round. They will indicate their ranking by using one of only three of their point placards—the 3, 4, or 5. That means a painting can score no less than fifteen and no more than twenty-five. As in previous rounds, judges will not know how their colleagues have voted.

"We're looking for a clear winner—the highest score, a second-place finisher, and a third-place finisher," Mellinger says. "If there is a tie for any of those positions, we will go to a tiebreaker. I can explain that procedure at that time, if it becomes necessary."

Before displaying the first entry, Adam Oswald's floating ruddy ducks, Mellinger cautions the audience that "especially at this point, it's very important not to have a crowd reaction to the voting on individual pieces, because we don't want to skew the judges' voting based on crowd reaction."

After passing Oswald's painting down the row of judges and giving the "Please vote" command, Mellinger waits for the panel's verdict:

3. 4. 3. 3. 3.

Sixteen. Not a strong showing, considering that the lowest number possible is fifteen.

Next up: Jim Hautman's pair of standing specklebellies, which sailed through the first round with five "In" votes and was the highest point-getter in the second round with twenty-four out of a possible twenty-five points. Hautman watches his painting being displayed for each judge, one after the other, from the dim upper reaches of the auditorium's steep rows of seats. He knows that strange things can happen. In the later rounds, judge fatigue and confusion become factors.

"And there's a random element to it," he'd said several months before. "I've seen twos become fives and fives become twos."

The white placards flash in the darkness.

4. 5. 5. 5. 5.

The twenty-four third-round points match the score he received in the second round. It's not the coronation Hautman got during the 1998 contest, when his flying scaup scored all fives in the final round and went on to win, but it's impressive.

The only judge who marks him down a point is Mike Chrisman, the square-jawed former California secretary of natural
resources.

Jim Hautman's status as the front-runner is even more solid
after the judges score the next three paintings. The pieces by
Sherrie Russell Meline, Russ Duerksen, and Dee Dee Murry
all generate lukewarm sixteens. Nearly half of the final eleven
paintings have been judged, and no one is even close to Hautman's score.

The sixth painting is Entry No. 96, the single standing specklebelly against the Western-looking Sutter Buttes painted by
Hautman's older brother Bob, who at the moment is baffled back
in Minnesota because something has gone awry with the live
streaming video. Due to sudden and unexpected technical difficulties, no one is able to track the voting on the Web.

"Please vote," commands Marie Strassburger, who is alter-
nating with Mellinger as the person who displays the paintings
to the judges. The judges raise their placards.

5. 5. 4. 5. 5.

The crowd's calculations are audible: Twenty-four. A tie.
The murmuring in the auditorium underscores the realization
that if no painting receives a higher score, then the two specklebelly paintings are assured first and second place.

The two Hautman brothers have finished one-two in the
Federal Duck Stamp Contest once before. That time, in 1994,
Jim placed first, and Bob took second. Jim says that his brother
graciously accepted the outcome.

"In the end, everybody wants to win," Jim says. "But if you
don't win, second place is the next best thing. And being second helps, too. Our names are linked, so if one of us does

something good, it sorta helps all the brothers as far as exposure and PR and all that stuff."

The painting that follows Bob Hautman's is different from the others in the final eleven, because it's the only painting that depicts a brant, that small, hardy, mostly black and white goose that migrates up and down the coasts of North America, from Alaska to Mexico's Baja peninsula in the West and from Massachusetts to North Carolina in the East.[1] Eighteen artists gambled on painting the relatively colorless brant for the 2010 contest, but only one entry, Kip Richmond's No. 127, has survived into the final round.

The father of three has been a professional artist for twenty years, and there's a spiritual bent to Richmond's website biography, which includes quotes from the book of Genesis and one from Aristotle that reads, "The aim of art is to represent not the outward appearance of things, but their inward significance."[2] He chose to place two of the birds—presumably a male and a female, although they're pretty much identical—among the tide pools of a rocky shore against the greenish backdrop of a crashing wave. The spirituality and inward significance of the birds is not immediately apparent, but the painting is a fine representation of the charisma-challenged geese.

Mellinger shows Richmond's painting to each judge in turn, then asks for their verdicts.

3. 5. 4. 3. 4.

The cumulative score of nineteen puts Richmond firmly in third position behind the tied Hautman brothers, with four paintings to go, including No. 177, Gerald Mobley's swimming shovelers—the entry Jim Hautman predicted less than an hour ago would be "the painting to beat."

Charles Shauck's swimming ruddy duck, No. 147, is next. It's strikingly similar to at least twenty-six other ruddy entries— the distinctive blue-billed duck on water, facing left, with a few reedy stems or just water in the background. And seven of the thirty-four paintings that made it into the second round had the same general composition. It's a fine painting, but perhaps the judges have seen too many like it.

4. 4. 3. 3. 3.

Seventeen. Not enough to break into the top three.

"Number 177," Mellinger announces—Mobley's pair of swimming shovelers, a drake and a hen moving from left to right across the frame, with just a hint of reedy stems against a dark-water background. Mobley seems to have embraced the rampant theory about a judging preference for simple backgrounds. Will it pay off?

Jim Hautman tenses as the painting he considers his most formidable challenger moves along the row of judges. He waits in the upper seats for them to raise their white scoring placards. If Mobley's birds score less than twenty-four, Hautman knows, he and his brother are increasingly likely to tie for first in this round, because there are only two paintings left to be judged. But there are other possibilities: What if Mobley scores twenty-four as well, creating a three-way tie? Or what if Mobley's painting scores a perfect twenty-five?

"Please vote," Mellinger says, and the placards rise.

3. 4. 3. 3. 4.

Seventeen.

Hautman allows himself to exhale, if only for a moment.

The next painting is Adam Grimm's flying shovelers. Its

brushwork is so detailed that the painting could be mistaken for the final photo composition that Grimm used to plan the piece. And the pose is memorable—one of Grimm's clear strengths as an artist—with the drake's right wing arcing almost protectively over the hen's back. In the frame, they fit together like a couple of nesting spoons.

3. 4. 4. 3. 3.

Another seventeen. The top three point-getters, Jim and Bob Hautman and Kip Richmond, remain unchallenged with just one painting left to judge: a pair of swimming Canada geese moving from right to left across the frame, with a few reeds as the only significant background.

"The last entry in Round Three is Number 222," Mellinger says, reverently holding up the piece by Rebecca Latham. The judges review it as carefully as the others, then vote.

4. 3. 3. 3. 3.

Sixteen.

An artist whose painting was eliminated in the second round, and who had correctly guessed the Hautman works, recaps what's going on. "Those brants are gonna finish third, and the Hautmans will finish first and second," he says. The judges are among the few people in the room who have no idea how many points each entry has received.

Mellinger steps back to the podium. "If the judges will bear with us, we'll verify the scores to see whether or not your work is done yet."

During the three minutes it takes the organizers to double-check the vote tallies, the sound of post-vote conversations and analysis builds in the auditorium until it reaches a sort of whispered roar. What are the odds of two paintings of speck-lebelly geese, those denizens of the Western flyway, ending up in a tie for first place?

Finally, Mellinger speaks again. "If I can have your attention: I suppose everybody in the audience knows this, but we ought to let our judges know that their work is *not* done. In fact, their most important work is not yet done. We have a tie between first and second place. So you still have to vote between the two top vote-getters to determine which entry will be the winner of the 2010 Federal Duck Stamp Contest and which piece will be the runner-up. We definitely have a third place. So in voting between these two pieces, you'll basically be choosing the winner and the second-place winner."

During the tiebreak process, entries No. 47 and No. 96—the first by Jim Hautman, the second by his brother Bob—will be shown to the judges together. Then the judges will once again be shown each painting on its own and asked to cast a final vote. Once again, they'll have placards with the numbers 3, 4, and 5 from which to choose. All previous scores have been set aside.

The tiebreak vote will be the only one that matters.

# THE LOOMING THREATS

O UTSIDE BERKELEY'S Brower Center, of course, the rest of the world is less focused on the Hautman brothers' impressive second-round scores, or even on the outcome of this vital but obscure federal art contest, than it is on the more pressing news of the day. The *San Francisco Chronicle* has written nothing about the contest since its June story predicting a showdown between the invading hunters and the local environmentalists. The Giants are about to begin a seven-game series against Philadelphia's Phillies for the National League Championship, and the 2010 midterm elections are just three weeks away. The paper has devoted much of its dwindling newsprint this weekend to previewing the baseball playoffs and reporting on preelection nonevents, including former Alaska governor and vice presidential candidate Sarah Palin's recent forty-minute speech to a conservative gathering in nearby San Jose.

The *Oakland Tribune*, based in the city adjacent to Berkeley, focuses its baseball passions on the hometown Athletics. It's less concerned about the Giants' chances in the playoffs. But it, too, aggressively ignores the unfolding drama of the Federal Duck Stamp Contest. On the first day of the contest judging, the *Tribune* publishes nothing about it, instead devoting the bulk of its front page to the protests of about fifty people who were arguing that the city's antigang injunction targeting the North Oakland and Fruitvale neighborhoods was a violation of the communities' civil rights.

The national media are equally disinterested. The contest is deemed unworthy of coverage in the *Wall Street Journal*, the *New York Times*, and *USA Today*. No TV camera crews or radio reporters prowl the venue. The only coverage is being generated by Duck Stamp Program officials themselves, including updates to the program's social media accounts and balky video of the contest available on the Fish and Wildlife Service website. A reasonable person might assume that the total audience numbers for that webcast will reach at least 235—the number of artists who have entered a painting in the 2010 contest. But according to artist Rob McBroom, who is monitoring the judging from his iPod Touch and a computer back home in Minnesota, the on-screen indicator showing the number of people watching the webcast has peaked at 115.

"Maybe I've just been spoiled by the glamour of other contest shows like *Miss USA* or *American Idol*," he says, "but am I wrong in thinking that watching it online is like C-SPAN2, but much, much less sexy?"

In any case, the media's aggressive lack of interest in the contest is of great concern to its organizers and ardent proponents. Among all of the looming threats to the program—and there are many these days—one of the most formidable is the general public's wholesale apathy toward it, especially among younger citizens. The increasingly intense efforts by program staff to counter that apathy offer a telling glimpse of their darkest fears not only for the future of their program but for the future of conservation and the overall vitality of American culture.

In April 2010, seven months before the contest judging in Berkeley, the brain trust of the Duck Stamp Program gathers, along with local and national representatives from the U.S. Fish and Wildlife Service, at St. Paul's Science Museum of Minnesota to stage the 2010 Junior Duck Stamp Contest, the climactic finish to a series of U.S. state and territorial contests put on by the federal program. The service started the annual junior contest in 1993 as part of a nature-themed educational program driven by the motto "Let's Go Outside!" The idea was to help bridge the widening gap between America's young people and the natural world.

The width of that gap is unintentionally apparent at the 2010 contest venue. The spectacular science museum is an impressive modern edifice, part of a downtown development that sits on a bluff overlooking the Mississippi River. And the dynamic operation inside the 370,000-square-foot building, with its 70,000 square feet of exhibit space, is clearly geared toward post-MTV generations raised on quick-cut, high-action video rather than something as seemingly archaic as the application of paint to canvas.

The day before the Junior Duck Stamp Contest is to begin, for example, the museum is featuring the forty-five-minute film *Arabia* in its Imax Convertible Dome Omnitheater. "Only the Omnitheater's giant screen can convey the stunning beauty of this exotic land, giving you a glimpse at a fascinating culture and way of life that has long been steeped in mystery," boasts the museum's website. Another highlight this weekend is the human-body exhibit, with its "Bloodstream Superhighway," which enables visitors to "see and feel the experience of blood pumping through veins with a 100-foot-long, two-inch diameter clear plastic tube"; "Body Hotel" where they can "use a magnifying glass and microscope to view a variety of organisms that can live on or in the human body"; and "a real human skeleton and actual thinly sliced sections of a real human body that show what a body's insides look like."

By contrast, the museum website's promotion of the Junior Duck Stamp Contest reads like a church-bulletin announcement, a dispassionate and lifeless echo from another era: "Come to the museum on Friday, April 23, to see who is chosen as the 2010 winner of the Junior Duck Stamp Contest. The judging ceremony will begin at ten a.m. and is open to the public at no cost."

At the museum's front desk the evening before the judging, a docent seems momentarily baffled by a request for directions to the Junior Duck Stamp Contest exhibit. "It's not 'til tomorrow, I don't think," he says, then gestures vaguely to an area far beyond the first-floor lobby. "But there were some people setting something up back there. You can go check."

In a rear corner of the museum's vast first floor, unannounced by any signs and lost among the museum's vastly more whiz-bang extravaganzas, is a small display manned only by a disinterested museum worker who has been posted to guard the top finishers of both the 2009 Federal Duck Stamp Contest and the previous year's junior contest. These are the *original* paintings by Robert Bealle, Jim and Bob Hautman, Scot Storm, and other past federal winners and finalists—the reigning elite of America's wildlife artists. The artworks are affixed to two small temporary walls that Duck Stamp Program staffers brought to Minnesota for the event. Two mesh ropes suggest that visitors keep a safe distance from the paintings, and a small sign reminds people not to touch.

But, of course, almost no one is there to touch them.

All in all, the whole thing feels anachronistic, completely out of phase with the times and the hyperactive museum scene in which it's nearly lost. It's a poignant reminder that the Federal Duck Stamp Program, which has been so vital to conserving millions of acres of wetlands and other wild areas for the nation's migratory waterfowl and other wildlife, is itself in danger of extinction.

In this get-it-now digital media age, the very notion of a paper stamp has a buggy-whip feel to it. Most kids today would no sooner collect stamps—or rocks, or coins, or baseball cards—than they would ride a nineteenth-century high-wheel bicycle to school. In some ways, that helps explain the high number of homeschooled kids among the approximately twenty-seven thousand students who participated in the state and territorial contests that led up to the 2010 federal junior contest. Presumably, those kids are less plugged into the youth culture that surrounds them. They still notice nature. They still go outdoors. They're still willing to paint a duck and compete for the chance to win the junior contest's first prize, a five-thousand-dollar-scholarship.

The program's efforts to reach out to America's young people have been going on for years, and in 2010 those efforts include a national contest for schoolkids to come up with an effective and memorable conservation slogan. The contest began many months ago, and one of the tasks of the junior contest judges is to choose the best slogan submitted. They settle unanimously on a submission from a young man in Arizona: "Wildlife speaks only the truth about our planet's future, but our greatest challenge is learning to listen."

Once the contest judging begins, it's easy to see the full extent of the effort to bring duck stamp awareness to a younger generation. Shortly before the ceremonies start, someone asks if the junior program, like the original program, notifies nonattending winners during a dramatic live phone call as soon as the voting is finished. No, someone else says, live calls don't work nearly as well in the junior contest as they do in the original one. Tom Melius, the duck-tie-wearing local regional director for the Fish and Wildlife Service, is only half joking when he suggests, "Maybe we should text them."

Organizers have wisely recruited Ian Leonard, the affable, fast-talking weatherman from Channel 9, the local Fox affiliate, to emcee the judging. In addition to keeping up a frothy stream of banter, Leonard tosses yellow rubber ducks into the crowd of about two hundred Minnesota schoolkids bused in to fill the museum's auditorium. He also frequently dips into his trove of waterfowl jokes to keep the kids engaged.

"Duck walks into a pharmacy and asks for some lip balm," Leonard says at one point, moving around the auditorium with a wireless microphone. "Pharmacist says, 'Will that be cash or check?' Duck says, 'Just put it on my bill!' "

The program itself is paced for speed so the attentions of the gathered kids won't stray while the judges winnow the fifty-one state and regional finalists to find a winner. In the end, Rui

"Raina" Huang, an eleventh grader from Bexley High School in Columbus, Ohio, walks away with the scholarship.

The program begins promptly at ten A.M. Despite a jam-packed schedule—welcoming remarks from Fish and Wildlife officials; a presentation of the flags and the Pledge of Allegiance, led by local Boy Scouts; a video lauding teachers for their role in promoting the contest and the presentation of awards to especially supportive teachers; and the introduction of the judges, an explanation of the judging process, and three rounds of judging—the whole thing is over by eleven.

If you hang around wildlife conservationists for a while, you'll notice how often the phrase "nature-deficit disorder" crops up in conversation. The phrase entered the vernacular in 2005 with the publication of journalist Richard Louv's book *Last Child in the Woods: Saving Our Children from Nature-Deficit Disorder*, an eventual bestseller that argues that direct exposure to nature is essential to a child's healthy physical and emotional development. The book begins with a memorable quote from a San Diego fourth grader ("I like to play indoors better 'cause that's where all the electrical outlets are")[1] and led to a national back-to-nature movement that rallied around the phrase "no child left inside."[2]

Louv argues that "it takes time—loose, unstructured dreamtime—to experience nature in a meaningful way" and suggests that America's parents have lost sight of that in their rush to steer their indulged progeny into organized activities such as dance lessons and youth sports. Pointing out that the trend has paralleled the complicated but alarming rise of obesity and physical malaise in American youth, Louv claims that the amount of time American children spent in organized sports increased by 27 percent between 1981 and 1997. "Demand for playing fields is up," he writes. "Expenditures on parks are falling. When parks are offered, the designers focus on reducing liability."

But when a park is graded to create a sports field, Louv argues, children lose the places where they once might have dipped their hands into a stream to catch a tadpole, heard the *cheep-cheep-cheeping* of a robin's hungry chicks, or kicked into an anthill just to see what would happen. "Research suggests that children, when left to their own devices, are drawn to the rough edges of such parks, the ravines and rocky inclines, the natural vegetation," he writes. "A park may be neatly trimmed and landscaped, but the natural corners and edges where children once played can be lost in translation."[3]

Adam Grimm, the South Dakota artist who won the Federal Duck Stamp Contest in 1999, says that humans used to be much more aware of the natural world. "But as people moved more and more into urban and suburban environments, it seems like they became more and more out of touch," he says.

For example, Grimm recalls hearing a recent news report about an unidentified "sea monster" that had washed up on a Massachusetts beach. "They were speculating it was a turtle without its shell. And I just laughed, because these are supposed to be smart people on the news. It's not like a cartoon, where a turtle can just crawl out of its shell. But they had no idea how a turtle is attached to its shell."

Grimm marvels when he hears about city dwellers who claim to have never seen a cow. "You know, like people in New York City," he says. "And I'm thinking, 'How have you never seen a real cow in real life? Even New Jersey has cows, so it's not like you have to go that far.' People are just very out of touch.'"

Brad Knudsen, the manager of the Patuxent Research Refuge, in Laurel, Maryland, says that his refuge often hosts events designed to help connect inner-city schoolkids with nature. At the wetland habitat, he enjoys watching nature work its special wonders. At first, he says, the kids are leery of getting anywhere near the mud or water in their "precious footwear." But after about forty-five minutes, he says, "there's actually peer pressure for them to get their shoes wet. It's really neat to see in just that short time. They're not afraid of it anymore."

On a more depressing note, he says he once invited members of the Environmental Club at historically black Howard University, in Washington, D.C., to visit the refuge for a walk in the woods. Knudsen says he was expecting about six or eight club members, but on the appointed day, the club organizer called to apologize. She could rally only two of the students to join them for the outing.

"I asked why, and she said some of them told her—and this is what she said; they're juniors in college—'I can't believe you're going out to see someone you just met and then going for a walk in the woods. You might not come back.' And she said others backed out because they were afraid of the woods. If your Environmental Club feels that way, what's going on? That really opened my eyes."

For generations, hunters have been the sustaining force of the Federal Duck Stamp Program, but like the number of stamp collectors, the number of hunters in the United States is dwindling. Fish and Wildlife Service figures released in 2007 show that the number of hunters sixteen and older declined by 10 percent between 1996 and 2006—from fourteen million to about twelve and a half million. The drop was most acute in New England, the Rocky Mountains, and the Pacific states, which lost four hundred thousand hunters in that span. While that might seem a plus to animal-welfare activists—the hunting numbers coincided with a 13 percent increase in wildlife watching—hunters historically are more likely than birders to pony up the money for habitat conservation.

The primary reasons for the drop, experts say, are the loss of hunting land to urbanization and a perception by many families that they can't afford the time or expenses that hunting requires. A spokesman for Ducks Unlimited told *USA Today*, "To recruit new hunters, it takes hunting families. I was introduced to it by my father, he was introduced to it by his father. When you have boys and girls without a hunter in the household, it's tough to give them the experience."[4]

Especially among children, the disconnect from nature is complicated by the rise in other diversions, primarily entertainment electronics. Television remains the "most effective thief" of a child's unstructured time, Richard Louv writes in an expanded and updated paperback version of his book released in 2008.[5] In that edition, he cites 2005 and 2006 studies conducted in association with the Kaiser Family Foundation that found that nearly one third of children from six months to six years of age lived in households where the TV was on all or most of the time. Most startling, children between the ages of eight and eighteen spent an average of nearly six and a half hours a day focused on a TV, a computer, a video game, or some other sort of electronic diversion, often more than one at a time—a reality that led the researchers to label today's kids Generation M, for "multitasking." "That's forty-five hours a week," Louv writes, "more time than once was considered an adult work week."

The Duck Stamp Program's Elizabeth Jackson, who coordinates the junior program, credits Louv's book with starting the national dialogue about the risks of distancing America's children from the natural world. But the book simply articulates what she has known for a long time and underscores the culture's general drift away from things she sees as vital.

"In a lot of ways, what I'm seeing mirrored in the school systems is also mirrored in the American way of life," Jackson says. "We're turning away from the outdoors, turning away from the arts. My fear is that we as a culture are turning away from a lot of things that are really, really essential."

Jackson says that the Florida coordinator of the Junior Duck Stamp Program, for example, told her that participation in the program was down in 2010 because some hard-pressed public school systems in her state had decided to offer physical education and arts programs for only half of the year, meaning that teachers had less time to introduce the Junior Duck Stamp Contest as part of the curriculum. "That's a mirror of what's really going on in our culture," Jackson says. "We're being driven by budgets, and we're not making time for these things."

Before you dismiss Jackson's comments as the self-interested lament of a federal bureaucrat trying to protect her program, consider the example of Bill Stewart of Chadds Ford, Pennsylvania, a thirty-three-year birder and chairman of the conservation committee of Delaware's Delmarva Ornithological Society.

Stewart says he goes birding in Delaware's national wildlife refuges—what he calls "the epicenter of shorebird migration" in America—at least fifty times a year. The marketing executive for a New York–based retail furniture company has no vested interest in protecting the Federal Duck Stamp Program and its youth-oriented offshoot beyond a core belief that the programs play a vital role in America's overall health.

On June 25, 2010, Stewart is attending the first-day-of-sale ceremony for the stamp made from Robert Bealle's wigeon, which won the 2009 contest. The ceremony is unfolding in the cavernous Bass Pro store in Hanover, Maryland, one of the many retail cathedrals to hunting and fishing that, like Cabela's and other outdoor-equipment retailers, seem to flourish especially well in the red-state landscape between the U.S. coasts.

The strategic partnership with Bass Pro is part of the Duck Stamp Program's efforts to sell the stamp in places other than post offices and to raise awareness of the program among hunters unaware of its history and critical role in conserving the wild areas where hunters pursue their sport. The alliance is one of two major program partnerships in the spring of 2010, the other being with Ducks Unlimited. Founded by waterfowl hunters in 1937, Ducks Unlimited boasts that eighty-six cents of every dollar it raises is used to conserve wildlife habitat[6] and has patterned its annual fund-raising efforts after the Duck Stamp Program by relying on art as a way to raise money and awareness about the need for conservation.

The Duck Stamp Program also partners at times with various regional birding, hunting, and conservation groups and events, such as North Dakota–based Delta Waterfowl, California Waterfowl, Minnesota-based Pheasants Forever, and the Waterfowl

Festival in Easton, Maryland. Years ago, the program had a partnership with the Peabody Hotel Group, which famously feature a daily parade of ducks through their lobby and into a fountain. But program chief Pat Fisher says that's no longer an active partnership: "As I recall, it mostly concerned the famous ducks marching in to start the federal contest, but it became too stressful and difficult for the ducks to travel after 9/11."

Stewart stands amid the Bass Pro store's displays of $119.99 motorized Canada goose decoys, $89.99 portable fish-cleaning tables, and $14.94 "Stars & Stripes Shirts" after receiving an award for his work as a private citizen to raise awareness about the Duck Stamp Program among nonhunters—an effort that began when the wording on the 1977–1978 stamp was amended from "hunting stamp" to "hunting and conservation stamp."

Stewart says he was stunned when he realized how few of his fellow birders owned a duck stamp. One of the initiatives he undertook with the 350-member Delmarva Ornithological Society was to start giving duck stamps as appreciation gifts to the people who led the society's birding expeditions. "So that's, like, thirty-five stamps right there that we buy," he says. "We also have them at our meetings for people to buy."

In the grand scheme, though, Stewart recognized that such a limited outreach effort to educate birders about the conservation value of the duck stamp wouldn't have much impact. So he approached the Duck Stamp Program staff and offered to do a series of public service ads for print magazines designed to spread the word. He enlisted the help of renowned Delaware wildlife photographer Kim Steininger and put together four ads built around the idea that the duck stamp isn't just a license for hunters or a self-interested way for them to maintain waterfowl populations so they can hunt them. The ads appeared in, among other publications, *Audubon* and *Birder's World*. "This year we need to branch out even further, continue to keep reaching out," Stewart says.

Fisher, the Duck Stamp Program's guiding light, understands that better than most. During dinner after the 2010 Junior Duck Stamp Contest in St. Paul, she allows herself to imagine an even more comprehensive and effective public service ad campaign that would enlist the biggest Hollywood celebrities, athletes, and other superstars of the day in an effort to preach the duck stamp gospel. At one point, she says, she had tried taking the message to the NASCAR crowd by recruiting 2002 Daytona 500 winner Ward Burton, a well-known advocate for land and wildlife conservation, to do a public service spot. Burton founded the Ward Burton Wildlife Foundation, which is involved in initiatives that range from renewable energy projects to government programs enabling landowners to ensure that their land is passed down for generations.

"I wanted him to put those 'Buy Duck Stamps' stick-ons on one of his cars," Fisher says, but that didn't work out.

A fellow diner suggests another name: Beyoncé.

"That was our thought too!" Fisher says. "We need a star who'll make people say, 'Oh my god, what was *that* about?' "

She ticks off the names of celebrities with a demonstrated passion for conservation and the environment. Robert Redford. Cameron Diaz. "I've always wanted to get Brett Favre— he's been a duck hunter all his life—to see if he'd be a spokesperson or do a PSA for us." Fisher says she has never approached the legendary NFL quarterback "because he has his own foundation, and he's really busy with football."

At this point, the forty-one-year-old Favre is still debating whether or not to return for yet another season. "When he retires," Fisher says, "I think we can go after him."

To the long list of realities working against the survival of the Federal Duck Stamp Program, the art contest that it spawned, and the endlessly fascinating subculture that grew up around it, add the simple fact that no one actually needs a physical duck stamp anymore. Buyers now can purchase an artless electronic equivalent of the duck stamp that's just as valid as a physical stamp emblazoned with an artist's rendering of a duck or goose, and as easy to obtain as the latest hit on iTunes. You can bet no one will be collecting, trading, or buying extras of those. Similarly, in California, home to the oldest state duck stamp program in the country, the state Department of Fish and Game has decided to stop requiring waterfowl hunters to affix the state stamp to their hunting license. It began printing the proof of purchase directly on the licenses and mailing out the actual stamps at the end of the hunting season. California Duck Stamps—whose designs also are the result of a nationwide art contest—were thus rendered an afterthought to the whole process.[7]

Of course, that sort of efficiency and convenience doesn't contribute in any way to the folkloric traditions of the Federal Duck Stamp Program and its state equivalents, which explains why Joe Hautman testified on July 21, 2005, before the U.S. House of Representatives' Committee on Natural Resources' subcommittee on fisheries and oceans. Hautman, the most comfortable public speaker among the three duck-stamp-painting brothers, had come to Washington to testify about H.R. 1494, the Electronic Duck Stamp Act of 2005, and H.R. 3179, the Junior Duck Stamp Reauthorization Amendments Act of 2005.

"Waterfowl hunters will purchase a 'stamp' regardless of its form," Hautman told the committee. "But with the electronic purchase some hunters could resent what would appear to be no more than an extra tax on their state hunting license. For many hunters, the traditional paper stamp is more than just a receipt for a tax paid, it is a badge of honor, a symbol of the hunter's respect for the natural resources they are privileged to use. Over the years, the duck stamp has inspired a loyalty and respect among hunters, not just for the program it represents, but also for the importance of wetlands conservation in general. Duck hunters are proud of their sport, proud of their heritage, and proud of *their* Duck Stamp Program."

Hautman permitted himself a moment during his testimony to recall his own introduction to the duck stamp. "Like so many people, I first learned about the duck stamp when I saw it, with its colorful and inspiring image, on my father's hunting license. I'm not sure that I would have asked about it, or learned to appreciate it, if it were only a number on a receipt."

Like Hautman, those who love the program almost invariably recall being drawn into the duck stamp subculture by the colorful artwork on the stamp on their father's old hunting licenses. Sometimes, though, there's more to the story.

Robert Bealle tells how the duck stamp tradition helps communicate conservation values and a hunter's responsibilities from generation to generation. He recalls the snowy day when his father suggested that they go duck hunting. Even though Bealle was only twelve—sixteen is the age at which hunters are first legally required to buy a Federal Duck Stamp—his father insisted on stopping at their local post office on the way into the field. "I said, 'Why are we stopping here?' And he said, 'You gotta have a duck stamp.' And he went in and bought a duck stamp and brought it out. I thought it was the neatest thing."

Bealle says his father told him to sign his name across the stamp, an old-school way of ensuring that hunters didn't share the nontransferable stamp. But the young Bealle refused to sign it.

"My dad said, 'You've got to. It's the law.' He always insisted on signing from corner to corner, right across it. But I didn't want to ruin it. I wanted to have it. I wanted to keep it. We had the biggest fight from there to the duck blind. We weren't gonna get out of that truck and into the blind until I signed across that stamp. I'm fifty-eight years old now, and I was twelve then. But I remember that as clear as can be."

Other duck stamp traditions are deeply interwoven into American culture. Bealle gives one precise example of what would be lost if the Duck Stamp Contest went away and paper stamps were replaced by electronic versions. "Ducks Unlimited will buy twenty seven hundred prints of my painting," he says. "It's at a very reduced rate, way below wholesale, like fifteen dollars apiece. But they'll send those prints to chapters all over the country and auction them off for several hundred dollars each. I also have to sign ten thousand of these little mini-sheets, and they sell for twenty-five dollars each, mostly to nonhunters. And all that money works hand in hand with the same [habitat conservation] projects the duck stamp money goes to. Well, if you don't have a duck stamp print to auction off, that money's gone."

And without paper stamps featuring bird art, Bealle points

out, the collector market for them will dry up as well. "You have collectors who buy whole sheets, eighty stamps on a sheet, and all that would be gone. You'd be down to just guys who buy the stamp to go hunting. That's all you'd have left."

Even that once was debated in Bealle's home state of Maryland, he says. A few years back, the state joined with the Fish and Wildlife Service in a pilot program offering waterfowl hunters the option of purchasing their federal duck stamp electronically, meaning that they no longer had to affix an actual duck stamp to their license. "A lot of guys would go in and buy two stamps, one to keep in mint condition and one to put on their license," he says. "Then they changed the law, just so they could keep the one stamp in mint condition. I told them, 'I thought the whole point was to make money, but now a guy who used to buy two, you're now only selling him one. What genius came up with this?'"

The gentleman farmer and 2009 contest winner pauses, then shakes his head. "I don't know about a society where you just throw away all the aesthetic things. Get rid of art? Music? We don't really *need* any of these things, but what kind of culture are you gonna have that has nothing aesthetic and no traditions?"

It doesn't help ease concerns about the duck stamp's future when, not long after the 2010 contest, President Obama introduces a federal budget that proposes to severely trim the amount of money used for habitat conservation efforts, sending those who care about habitat conservation into doomsday mode. While the preliminary budget doesn't propose cuts to the Duck Stamp Program itself, it does suggest sobering cuts to the land acquisition efforts that the program has always helped support.

In an action alert from Ducks Unlimited released the same day as the federal budget proposal, CEO Dale Hall claims that the proposed cuts would significantly undermine the ability of state agencies, private conservation organizations, and individual farmers, ranchers, and other landowners to partner with the federal government to conserve waterfowl habitat. In particular, he says that the budget cuts would eliminate nearly forty-eight million dollars in North American Wetlands Conservation Act grants and ninety million dollars in wildlife grants to states, and would cut by 81 percent the budget for conservation land acquisitions in the Prairie Pothole Region.

Cuts that severe, Hall writes, "would cripple conservation efforts as we know them."

## THE HUNTER-HUGGER SCHISM

As the prime movers of American wetlands conserva-tion gradually narrow their focus to the two remaining Hautman paintings throughout the weekend of October 15 and 16, 2010, the complicated relationship between hunting and conservation is perfectly expressed on a high-rise four-wheel drive rumbling along the Bay Area freeways. It's not the cushy ride of a suburban SUV jockey who'll never encounter terrain more rugged than a supermarket speed bump. The road scars and bumper stickers signal that this is the vehicle of a dedicated hunter. One back-window decal signifies the truck owner's membership in Ducks Unlimited. An unrelated sticker on the vehicle's rear bumper simply reads, "If it flies, it dies."

These two seemingly contradictory notions of waterfowl management—habitat conservation and waterfowl hunting—aren't easily reconciled, or even tolerated, by birders, hikers, and other outdoors enthusiasts. Those people, the ones Fish and Wildlife deputy director Dan Ashe identifies as the "noncon-sumptive conservationists," are the ones the Federal Duck Stamp Program desperately needs in order to continue its good work.

And that's the biggest challenge facing the program today:

Unless it can convince birders and other nonhunters that buying duck stamps is the best way to conserve wetlands and the
other wildlife habitats they treasure, the burden of doing so
will continue to fall to the dwindling number of hunters and
stamp collectors who traditionally have supported the program.

Trace that line to its logical conclusion, and eventually you
get to the end of the grandest idea in the history of wildlife
conservation.

Many nonhunting nature enthusiasts remain unaware of the
Duck Stamp Program. "If you explain it to them, they'll buy it,"
says Junior Duck Stamp Program overseer Elizabeth Jackson.
"But our particular challenge is helping those folks understand
what duck stamp dollars do, because with birders there's the
misconception that it's a hunting stamp. Yes, true, but while it's
a hunting stamp, it protects the same wildlife."

Artist Robert Bealle has little patience with those who dismiss hunters as bloodthirsty pillagers of the natural world. If
you listen to the lifelong hunter for any length of time, you
hear a man who understands nature on a deeper and more profound level than most. Bealle literally knows waterfowl from
the inside out, having once identified the migration route of
a bird he had shot by linking the undigested aquatic vegetation
in its crop—an exotic, non-native species called hydrilla—to a
particular stretch of the Potomac River. (He also says he could
taste the difference in the duck meat when the canvasbacks he
hunts began feeding on little clams in the Patuxent River.)

"It makes me mad when I hear people say hunters save ducks
to shoot ducks. That's just not true," says Bealle, whose business
card identifies him as "legendary outdoorsman, wildlife artist
extraordinaire, gentleman farmer, all-around nice guy."

In the overall mission of wildlife conservation, Bealle sees ducks and geese as the equivalent of the doe-eyed puppies in those adopt-a-pet ad campaigns—the kind of creatures whose mass public appeal can both tug at heartstrings and loosen purse strings. Ducks and geese are like the glamour players on a football field, he says. "Nobody really focuses that hard on the other players; they focus on the standouts. When you're talking about an ecosystem or wetlands, nobody really cares about the spotted toad and this and that and whatever else lives there. But when you have a program that protects the wetlands with duck stamp money, look at all the other things it takes to make a sustainable ecosystem that's now protected. You put it off-limits so the ducks can go there, but it's also off-limits so somebody can't drain it and kill off all the frogs and salamanders and cattails."

Hunters have borne the burden of conserving such ecosystems, Bealle says, and have done so willingly since they began buying duck stamps in 1934. He says this as a matter of fact, not as a complaint. "Hunters put more money back into conservation than a lot of these other people and antihunters . . . Who shows up at Ducks Unlimited banquets and spends thousands of dollars on an auctioned gun they could have bought for four hundred dollars over the counter?"

Jason Parsons, an Illinois native who became the first winner of the Junior Duck Stamp Contest in 1993, laments that nonhunters' fundamental misunderstanding of hunting culture is limiting America's ability to conserve its wetlands and other wild places. He was born into that culture, and he depended on hunting in the 1980s when the economy turned down and his father lost his job. "We grew our own produce. We trapped in the winter. We hunted and fished for our food, and we stocked our freezers with it."

And he was taught to take care of the land where he and his family were permitted to hunt. "We picked up the garbage. We made sure nobody was poaching, or that we didn't take more than the law said we could. And whether you're a hunter or you're an eco-friendly tree hugger or whatever you want to call an antihunter, truly it's just a basic respect for the environment, you know?"

Parsons sees hunting and the art that celebrates it in the broader context of culture. Along with Bealle, he helped judge the Junior Duck Stamp Contest in St. Paul in April 2010. And at one point, as the judges gathered in an upstairs staging area of the Science Museum of Minnesota, Parsons and Bealle—who had never met before—disappeared into a long, animated conversation with another judge about their hunting experiences. The bond between the men was obvious as they regaled one another with stories from the field. The thirty-three-year-old Parsons later explains that "what you saw right there is a certain type of a culture. I can sit down with a fifty-eight-year-old man and a seventy-year-old man and share stories because we all know that culture and lifestyle. We grew up in it. I learned how to respect a gun because of what my dad and grandpa taught me."

He insists that hunting and wildlife art are no less a part of American culture than jazz. "It's those creative outlets that really, truly define us as a culture. And wildlife art is one of those outlets."

Still, there's no point in denying that hunters have an image problem. William Webster, the spry eighty-four-year-old from

Frontenac, Minnesota, who founded the outdoor lifestyle retailer Wild Wings and remains one of the world's leading duck stamp collectors, suggests that the advantage America's fishermen have over its hunters, in terms of public image, is the catch-and-release ethic often demonstrated on those sport-fishing programs on cable TV. For the most part, that ethic takes death out of the equation.

Unfortunately, Webster notes, there's no real equivalent in hunting.

But the inconvenient truth for those conservationists who decry hunting is that the number of birds killed by hunters each year is minuscule when compared to the other fates that await birds in the wild. According to a mortality chart that ornithologist and field guide author and illustrator David Allen Sibley created from various sources in 2003 and posted on his website, annual waterfowl hunts kill about 15 million birds a year in North America. By contrast, as many as 976 million birds die each year by crashing into windows. Domestic and feral cats kill at least 500 million. Hunters don't even kill as many birds as are claimed annually by high-tension wires (174 million), pesticides (72 million), cars (60 million), and communication towers (up to 50 million).

Dying birds make dramatic TV footage during catastrophes such as the massive oil spill in the Gulf of Mexico in the spring of 2010, but according to Sibley's figures, such spills are among the least significant factors in overall bird mortality, right down there with electrocution and death by wind turbine. Avian mortality rates are raised, too, by occasional and mysterious bird die-offs such as the one that happened in Beebe, Arkansas, on December 31, 2010, when thousands of red-winged blackbirds seemingly dropped dead from the sky. State wildlife officials advanced a theory that the birds were startled to death by New Year's Eve fireworks, or perhaps died through their own clumsy attempts to flee them.

Emphasizing that habitat destruction is the single biggest threat to bird populations, Sibley also notes that "studies of hunting have documented that in certain cases killing small numbers of birds can *improve* the health and survival of the remaining birds. As long as the habitat is intact, the population has the potential to replace the lost birds."[1]

Amy K. Hooper, the editor of the Southern California–based *WildBird* magazine, agrees with the assessment of the Duck Stamp Program's Elizabeth Jackson that the birding community has a fundamental lack of awareness about duck stamps and their importance to habitat conservation. She tries to bring up the topic as often as possible on her blog, WildBird on the Fly, and often includes a homemade public service ad that promotes duck stamps in issues of the print magazine.

Hooper says that animosity between hunters and birders plays out on social media networks such as Facebook, as well as in everyday discussions. "Conversations with birders about the program involve a lot of education and trying to bridge that gap between hunters who shoot birds and people who look at them. It can be pretty interesting."

She describes the intensely hostile vibe that arises when, say, camouflage-wearing hunters walk into a restaurant full of birders. "Birders tend to be negative and condescending toward hunters. They allow stereotypes to affect their view, and there's an us-versus-them mentality that's very strong for some folks."

Hooper tries to temper the resentment by pointing out to her readers that hunters have to buy the Federal Duck Stamp every year if they're going to participate in their activity, and that ninety-eight cents of every duck stamp dollar goes to conserving acreage that directly benefits birders. "And I try to work in the idea that hunters are working within limits set by biologists. It's not this willy-nilly destructive thing that a lot of birders think of as hunting. You have qualified biologists setting these limits [on the number of birds a hunter can take], but a lot of people don't think of that."

She's not optimistic about convincing birders to embrace the idea expressed by Fish and Wildlife's Dan Ashe, who argues that bird-watchers should develop a community ethic that encourages birders to buy and display a duck stamp. "There's just a cultural bias against anything related to hunting," she says.

The *WildBird* editor adds that birders sometimes argue that they shouldn't have to pay fees or buy duck stamps because their hobby doesn't consume anything. "True, they're not taking a bird away," she says. "But they're not considering the impact their vehicle has on that site, or the maintenance of the trails that they're walking on."

Debate about the hunter-hugger schism rages mostly in the blogosphere. In a 2009 posting to the blog 10,000 Birds,[2] for example, amateur naturalist Mike Bergin of Rochester, New York, argued that the government doesn't value the conservation efforts of birders as much as those of hunters. He wrote, "When it comes time to draft important conservation legislation or plan the creation of a 21st Century Youth Conservation Corps, we non-extractive wildlife enthusiasts are forgotten in favor of the hook and bullet club . . . The duck stamp is a hunting license. It seems to me that hunters are credited for the funds flowing from the sale of said stamp despite the major push among American birders to purchase it for conservation."

Bergin suggested that some sort of "refuge access pass" for birders might be more appropriate than urging them to buy duck stamps, and might help more clearly establish the contributions that birders make toward the overall conservation effort.

But birders such as Bill Stewart of Delaware's Delmarva Ornithological Society aren't too concerned about who gets credit. Stewart sees the Duck Stamp Program as a treasure at risk. "The duck stamp has an identity crisis," says the deeply tanned outdoorsman. "There's anywhere between forty-eight million and seventy-two million birders in America. It's the fastest-growing outdoor leisure activity. But most people who are not hunters don't have any idea what the duck stamp is. They think it's for hunters only. But once birders understand that it's a conservation stamp, they readily buy them."

There's evidence that word about the conservation value of duck stamps is spreading among those in the birding community. According to the Fish and Wildlife Service, about 10 percent of duck stamp revenue now comes from nonhunters, including stamp collectors, art dealers, and wildlife enthusiasts.[3] But just days after the August deadline to submit paintings for the 2010 Federal Duck Stamp Contest, a former president of the Delmarva Ornithological Society posted a provocative item on his blog.[4]

In that post, Jeffrey A. Gordon recalled buying a duck stamp at the visitor center at Delaware's 15,978-acre Bombay Hook National Wildlife Refuge. The volunteer who sold it to him asked if he planned to use the stamp for hunting and dutifully recorded his "No" answer in a logbook behind the counter. Curious, Gordon asked how many of the duck stamp buyers during the previous month had identified themselves as nonhunters. Of the 114 stamps sold, the volunteer reported, all but nine had been sold to nonhunters.

"Yes, that's right," Gordon wrote. "Just over ninety-two percent were sold to non-hunters. Of course, this is nothing like a definitive survey. Not every non-hunter is a birder. And I would guess that hunters would be much better represented at other outlets where stamps can be purchased. But still, I couldn't help but feel just a little bit proud."

# JUDGMENT DAY:
# THE TIEBREAK ROUND

T HE AUDITORIUM OF the Brower Center is absolutely silent as the judges prepare to review the two remaining paintings. Larry Mellinger, the charmingly bureaucratic attorney from the Interior Department's Office of the Solicitor, announces that they'll first assess No. 47. The judges have no idea who painted it, of course, but by now many others in the room know that the pair of standing specklebellies against dramatic gray storm clouds is the work of three-time winner Jim Hautman. As Mellinger moves with the original painting down the row of five judges, each judge in turn leans forward for a final look.

"Please vote," Mellinger says, and the placards flash.

4. 5. 5. 3. 5.

Twenty-two.

Judge Mike Chrisman, who gave Hautman's geese the only four rating among its otherwise perfect scores during the third round, proves consistent with another four in the tiebreak round. But judge John Eadie, who rated the painting a five during the third round, has inexplicably dropped his score to a three in the tiebreak vote, prompting a murmur among the crowd's most ardent handicappers.

"Thank you," Mellinger says.

Next up is Entry No. 96, the solitary specklebelly goose that Bob Hautman decided to set against a backdrop of central California's Sutter Buttes, hoping to subtly influence a judging panel he correctly assumed would have a distinctly Western skew. Seeing the two finalists for the top prize in such quick succession, some in the room realize for the first time that the only two surviving paintings feature the exact same species—and one of the year's least popular species, at that. What are the odds?

Back in Delano, Minnesota, Bob Hautman has no idea that his painting is vying for first place with the entry by his brother Jim. The technical difficulties that earlier interrupted the live streaming webcast of the Duck Stamp Contest finals judging still have not been resolved. Despite the best efforts of the contest organizers to take the event worldwide, none of the one hundred or so people trying to watch it from afar can, at this critical moment, see a thing.

The five judges lean forward again as assistant Marie Strassburger presents Bob Hautman's painting to each of them.

"Please vote," she says. For the last time during the 2010 contest, the white placards rise.

5. 4. 3. 5. 4.

Twenty-one.

Judges Chrisman and Eadie clearly prefer Bob Hautman's single specklebelly. Judges Vecchiarelli, Serie, and Garcia clearly prefer Jim Hautman's pair. Just that quickly, it's over.

Everyone in the room knows there's a one-point difference in the total scores, except for the five judges and Jim Hautman, who will later recall that he was "too nervous to add right" and had no idea that, for the fourth time, he was about to be announced as the official winner of the Federal Duck Stamp Contest. He's conferring with friends, wondering, when Mellinger steps to the microphone.

"Judges, I can let you know that you're about done." The crowd breaks into relieved applause. "And now, you and the rest of the world will find out just what you did."

The attorney steps back, allowing Fish and Wildlife officials to take over. Jerome Ford, the deputy assistant director of Fish and Wildlife's Migratory Bird Program, thanks Mellinger and others and then again introduces Dan Ashe, his boss.

Ashe gets right to it, announcing that the third-place winner is North Carolina's Kip Richmond, whose name is not particularly well-known in the duck stamp world. There's a moment of what seems like confused silence, then the crowd breaks into a round of enthusiastic applause. But the judges still look confused. They don't know which painting was Richmond's, and several ask to see it again.

"What's the number?" one of them asks.

"Is it the brant?" another asks and is told that it is.

The moment speaks to the basic integrity of the contest. How could anyone possibly fix a contest in which the judges themselves are the last to know the final results?

"The second-place winner is a name that's familiar to all of us," Ashe says. "Robert Hautman."

The audience applauds again. Up in the peanut gallery, Jim Hautman stops his nervous ciphering. He is, as he will recount later, "shaking as bad as [he's] ever shaken."

Ashe clears his throat. "The first-place winner, and the winner of the 2010–2011 Federal Duck Stamp competition, is James Hautman."

The crowd erupts. If there's any resentment among the attending artists because of the one-two Hautman sweep, any sense that the brothers are getting more than their fair share of the glory, it's not apparent in the sustained and sincere applause. At least this year, the two competing Hautman brothers were *that* good.

Jim Hautman, wearing jeans and a black pullover with the sleeves pushed up to his elbows, descends the auditorium stairs like a man being coaxed from a ledge. Ashe shakes his hand, and the winner warily steps to the microphone, as if it might bite his nose.

"Thank you all very much," Hautman begins. "I'll tell you what, this just leaves you speechless. I've been, ah . . . My dad started collecting duck stamps in '34, and every year up till World War Two he only missed a few. And it's just always been a lifelong dream of mine. And, ah, you know, I've won it before, and it's tough to breathe out there during these things. But thank you very much to the judges, of course. I can't say 'Great job,' because that sounds a little bit self-congratulatory."

Hautman looks relieved. Maybe it's because he has become more comfortable speaking in public since his first win, at age twenty-five, in 1989. Or maybe it's because, despite his impressive record of three previous wins, the last twelve years without a victory have felt like an interminable dry spell for someone so focused and driven to succeed. He pauses, then continues.

"And I just also have to thank my friends and family for their support, especially my wife, Dorothy. This is the first entry in five years that she's given me a thumbs-up on." When the audience's laughter subsides, he adds, "She's got a good eye."

The winning artist then turns his attention to the other artists in the room. "I know we're all fiercely competitive, but there's a certain camaraderie we share, and I appreciate their friendliness." He wraps up his comments by thanking everyone involved with the Duck Stamp Program, which he says he's looking forward to representing once again.

Hautman steps back from the microphone. Jerome Ford steps forward and announces that the stamp featuring Hautman's winning painting will go on sale in June 2011. He urges everyone in the room "to put your stamp on conservation" by buying one.

Almost immediately, the AV guy cues up a recording of the song that's played each year to conclude the proceedings. Holding his winning painting, Jim Hautman is quickly surrounded by judges, D.C. dignitaries, and others who want their picture taken with the 2010 Federal Duck Stamp Artist. The absurdist strains of the 1976 No. 1 *Billboard* hit "Disco Duck" fill the Brower Center auditorium.[1]

After most of the well-wishers have filtered away, Hautman sits down in one of the auditorium's front-row seats. He seems as low-key as ever, but confesses that his nerves are shot.

"This year was a little different, because it looked like I was going to win after the third round," he says. "But I'll tell you what, at the very end that whole tiebreaker business just about did me in. I was too nervous to add right, and I didn't even know."

Robert Bealle, the outgoing Federal Duck Stamp Artist, approaches like a kid who wants an autograph. He has crossed paths with Hautman only once before, and as a man who measured his talent against the Hautman brothers for two decades before finally winning, he's behaving like someone in the presence of royalty. Bealle compliments Hautman on the "fantastic" composition of his winning piece and can't resist telling Hautman how he felt the previous year when he realized that his wigeon painting had—in that glorious, possibly once-in-a-lifetime moment—bested the best.

"The fact that ya'll were in there, and I won, I mean, who would want to win if none of the Hautmans were in the contest?" Bealle says. "It'd be like being in the Super Bowl but playing a high school team or something. So that just made it . . . The fact that you and your brother come in first and second this year, and I'm sandwiched right in there, I'm thinking maybe this is a big deal."

Bealle offers to share some of the business contacts and information he has picked up during his year as the Federal Duck Stamp Artist, and the two men part just as Dorothy Hautman approaches and says she has heard there's a reception upstairs.

Before they leave the auditorium, though, Jim Hautman thinks about how his next conversation with brother Bob might go. This is the ninth first-place win since 1989 for one of the three competing Hautman brothers. And finishing second is certainly nothing to be ashamed of—Bob won in 1996 and 2000 and has finished second once before.[2] The problem, of course, is that the year of that second-place finish, the artist who bested him was . . . Jim.

Now it has happened again.

Jim Hautman, the newly crowned 2010 Federal Duck Stamp Artist, leans in close. "He's gonna kill me when I get home."

Postmortem analysis begins immediately in the lobby of the Brower Center, and except for a few discouraged grumbles from overlooked artists, the whole scene unfolds like a congenial church social. The one-two Hautman finish is a stunning affirmation of the brothers' talent, just as Kip Richmond's unexpected third-place finish underscores the treasured notion that relative unknowns have a legitimate shot at winning it all. Everyone seems to agree that the drama of the tiebreak vote was thrilling, and that the two Hautman paintings stood out from the field. At least in the immediate postgame analysis, no one makes much of the possibility that the subtle Western flavor of the paintings that finished first, second, and third—all featuring geese that range up and down the West Coast of the United States—influenced a judging panel drawn mostly from California.

There's also general consensus that the judges were especially unforgiving during the first round, when they voted only 34 of the 235 entries through to the second round. Even one of the judges wonders if perhaps the contest and the Duck Stamp Program might have benefited from a less brutal first cull.

"In retrospect, maybe I might have said, 'Let's get a lot of people through the first round so they feel good about it,'" judge John Eadie says. "That may be something they want to think about, and maybe something they could direct the judges [on]. You know, 'Let's don't worry too much about the first round. Try to get ones that really aren't going to be appropriate through.' That might encourage more buying [of stamps] and more engagement [with the program]. But I feel if it's not going to make it into the final round, then why prolong it?"

Eadie also endorses the idea of staging the contest in different parts of the country. "Berkeley—what a great choice if they're trying to broaden the scope of the Duck Stamp Program," he says. "We can go back to the same old places and the same old crowds, just the duck stamp artists and the stamp collectors and so forth, but if we want to bring in the public, and we want it to be a hunting *and* a conservation stamp, it's a great idea to move it around the country and get more people engaged in this fabulous program."

Having witnessed the judging process firsthand, Eadie offers that every step of it, from the backroom discussions to the public voting, is "squeaky clean," and that with assigned waterfowl expert Thom Lewis's help, the panel paid keen attention to matters of anatomical and biological correctness. One of the contenders featuring a brant triggered a spirited discussion about the positioning of one of the bird's legs, which Eadie found "sort of funky. It was a good piece of work, but it couldn't have existed" that way in real life.

Richmond's pair of seaside brant apparently ended up in third place because the judges began questioning the anatomical proportions of artist Sherrie Russell Meline's Canada goose, which initially was among their favorites. "It was a really nice composition," one judge says later, "but it was weird. The back, the wings were off, and it seemed like the neck was kind of short."

Judges dinged artists for depicting flight feathers "that were splaying when they shouldn't have been splaying" and for painting a ruddy duck with a yellow eye. One judge marked Richmond's brant down because a spray of sea foam behind the geese detracted from the focus on the birds. Another felt that Bruce Miller's swimming shoveler was "a little painterly," apparently the kiss of death in a contest where winners tend to be as sharp and detailed as a *National Geographic* photograph.

In the final analysis, Eadie says, hunters and those who have spent countless hours in marshes and wetlands observing bird behavior will always have an advantage over those who are less familiar with birds in the wild.

"It's one thing to say, 'Yes, that's how the bird looks,'" he says. "But you have to know how it feels when the bird is coming in, and if it just doesn't feel right, you can pick up on that. You don't necessarily have to be a hunter, but I don't think you can just paint from photographs and really get it right for the duck stamp. A lot of the paintings are birds that you typically see in hunting situations, so you get that perspective. And I think if one wants to be really successful as a duck stamp artist, you need to see that, feel that, to understand what is a natural pose, or attitude, or flight pattern."

Artist Mark Berger, the analytical aerospace engineer from Southern California, approaches some of the judges after the winners have been chosen and asks for a little post-contest analysis of his painting of two Canada geese in flight. Judge Joe Garcia tells him that "the legs seemed a little heavy," an opinion later echoed by Eadie, who also found the position of the lead goose's legs a bit awkward.

"It just doesn't look like a bird that's coming in to land," Eadie says. "Mark said, 'But that was from a photograph, so it's true.' Well, OK. Technically, it may be correct, and it may have been what the bird was doing, but compositionally, it just didn't work."

The difference between first and second place—between Jim Hautman's stormy pair of specklebellies and his brother Bob's lone specklebelly standing against the Sutter Buttes—apparently came down to several judges' perception that the single bird was "a little too stately and not quite as dramatic," according to someone who was in the judging green room before the tie-breaker round. Eadie, whose late-stage voting clearly reflected his preference for Bob Hautman's singleton over Jim Hautman's pair, concedes that Bob's choice of the Sutter Buttes was smart and that his ultimate preference for that painting may have been influenced by its Western landscape.

Upstairs, federal and regional Fish and Wildlife staffers, judges, artists, and invited guests parse the results over wine and tray-passed hors d'oeuvres. Then it's time to announce the winner of the day's second-most-watched contest.

Twenty of the visitors who earlier cast paper ballots at the Brower Center's reception table for the chance to win a pair of field binoculars guessed that Jim Hautman's painting would triumph. A reception organizer randomly draws a ballot from one of those twenty and unfolds the piece of paper, then steps up to a microphone to announce, after a confused pause, that Jim Hautman has won that, too.

*14*

# WHERE THE WILD THINGS ARE

EXCEPT FOR THE two old-school ladies' hatboxes in his hands, Kirk Gilligan looks much like any other manager of one of the nation's 553 national wildlife refuges on this Saturday morning about three months after the 2010 Duck Stamp Contest finals. He has the trim physique of a dedicated outdoorsman, and he's outfitted head to toe in U.S. Fish and Wildlife Service brown, his baseball cap and light jacket bearing the service's distinctive logo. He's preparing to lead about twenty-five visitors—an amiable mix of retirees, Cub Scouts, binoculars-toting birders, and a few curious souls—on a two-and-a-half-hour tour of the saltwater marsh known as the Seal Beach National Wildlife Refuge.

The refuge Gilligan manages is different from all the others, though, and not just because it's one of the few national wildlife refuges amid the incomprehensible sprawl of Southern California's five counties. True, its 965 estuary acres sit in northwestern Orange County like a carefully managed island of tranquillity within the acid-creep of urbanization about twenty-five miles south of downtown Los Angeles, between Seal Beach and Sunset Beach. In the late nineteenth century, the Anaheim Bay and nearby Bolsa Chica wetlands areas were home to twenty-three duck-hunting clubs. Today, what remains of that wilderness is surrounded by freeways, concrete-corralled rivers, office buildings, industrial facilities, and the dense residential communities along the coast. Amid the urban clutter, the refuge's meandering channels of Anaheim Bay saltwater, empty islands, and startling absence of roads look, from above, like a mapmaker's mistake or an inexplicable smudge on a satellite photo. (It's easy to get a view from above; the refuge lies directly beneath the path of jetliners landing at nearby Long Beach Airport.)

But the National Wildlife Refuge System includes plenty of lovely wildlife way stations amid the chaos of large American cities. What makes Seal Beach different from the others is that it also sits in the middle of the five-thousand-acre Seal Beach Naval Weapons Station, where about half of the ships from the U.S. Navy's Pacific Fleet—cruisers, destroyers, frigates, and medium-size amphibious assault ships—come to be loaded with missiles, torpedoes, and other ordnance. Seeing the refuge is not simply a matter of paying an entry fee or flashing a current duck stamp, which grants free access to the system's other refuges. At Seal Beach, snagging a spot on the once-a-month tour requires both a reservation and, especially since September 11, 2001, proper identification.

Gilligan sets the hatboxes down on a bench outside the refuge's tiny welcome center, the brick outer walls of which feature faded murals of pelicans and other local wildlife. Other refuges have elegant visitor centers, such as the one at Minnesota Valley, in Minneapolis, which looks like a ski lodge and includes a 125-seat auditorium, a bookstore, and an innovative geothermal-and-solar heating system, or the National Wildlife

Visitor Center at Maryland's Patuxent Research Refuge, which looks like the convention center of a progressive midsize city. By contrast, the one at Seal Beach looks like a converted post–World War II navy mail room that's been tarted up by dedicated volunteers, which is what it is.

Gilligan kicks things off with a brief history lesson about the refuge. The naval weapons station was commissioned in 1944, just a year before the end of World War II. But Southern California was about to be transformed in ways that few had ever imagined. The war had brought legions of soldiers and sailors to the area for training or deployment. While here, many had fallen in love with the temperate climate, beach culture, fruit trees, and general ease of living, so after the war, many decided to come back. The resulting population boom meant a crushing need for housing, services, and roads; California was on its way to becoming the nation's most populous state, with nearly thirty-seven million residents and countless more undocumented immigrants calling it home in 2010. One proposal back then would have extended Interstate 605—a major north-south freeway that runs mostly along the San Gabriel River from Irwindale to Seal Beach—right through the estuary.

"Right about where we're standing," Gilligan says.

He stops the history lesson to point out that, thanks to that population boom, only about 5 percent of California's coastal marshes still exist. Referring to the birds and other creatures that rely on those wetlands, he underscores the problem by asking, "How would you survive on five percent of your salary, and in five percent of your habitat?"

Determined to stop the freeway expansion plan, the navy designated the estuary a Navy Wildlife Refuge in 1964. Six years later, the navy, the California Department of Fish and Game, and the U.S. Fish and Wildlife Service entered into a three-way agreement to preserve and protect the estuary's fish and wildlife. Unfortunately, the agreement was toothless. None of its three partners had the authority to stop the freeway plan. By then, though, public opposition to it had taken root, and in 1972, with the help of a local congressman and a state senator, the navy refuge became a part of the National Wildlife Refuge System.

Gilligan explains that refuges within that system gain the considerable protection and power of the federal government, wielded on behalf of the refuge's vulnerable wildlife. Why? "Does anybody remember what was going on in fashion around the turn of the twentieth century?" he asks.

Gilligan reaches down and lifts the lid from one of the hatboxes, a round one labeled with the elegant script logo of a long-defunct shop called Dorée. Into the morning's bright sunlight he lifts a pillbox hat, its outer surface a crazy quilt of patterns. When several tour members realize that those patterns were created by overlaying hundreds of feathers, seemingly from a ring-necked pheasant, they gasp—a typical reaction, Gilligan says. He reaches down again and removes the lid of a six-sided hatbox from a shop called Passeys in nearby Lakewood. This time he lifts out an even more elaborate hat, a pink-tinged number with a wide brim decorated with the primary plumage of what likely was a healthy, breeding roseate spoonbill, one of the most striking birds in North America.

Spoonbills—large wading birds that thrive in the southeastern U.S. coastal states—once were driven to near extinction by professional plume hunters. By the 1930s, only thirty to forty breeding pairs were left in the entire state of Florida, sole survivors of a massacre to satisfy the demand for feathers to decorate ladies' hats and fans.[1]

Gilligan has been using the hats as teaching tools since he started working at the refuge in 2006. As beautiful as they are, they trigger an undeniable gag reflex among serious conservationists, who see in them what animal rights activists might consider the moral equivalent of apparel made from mink or chinchilla pelts. "They're a good way to show our visitors something tangible about how wasteful our society was with regards to wildlife resources back then, and toward birds in particular," the refuge manager explains. "I think it also helps folks to remember why and how the refuge system was born."

On a high wall above the "Wisdom of Wildness" section at the National Wildlife Visitor Center at Maryland's Patuxent Research Refuge is a stenciled quote from aviation pioneer and conservationist Charles Lindbergh: "The human future depends on our ability to combine the knowledge of science with the wisdom of wildness."

But the term "wildness" can be a little misleading when referring to much of America's wildlife. It ignores the staggering amount of intense forethought and management that goes into keeping the nation's wild places and their inhabitants healthy.

The Seal Beach refuge, for example, was established to provide protected habitat for threatened species such as the California brown pelican, the peregrine falcon, and the Belding's savannah sparrow and, especially, for the endangered light-footed clapper rail and California least tern. After migrating from their winter homes in Central and South America, least terns come back to their Seal Beach refuge between March and midsummer. Their nesting area is a tiny island of sand, called NASA Island, in the middle of the massive naval weapons station. Gilligan and his team have built fences around the sand island to keep ground predators away, and the Friends of Seal Beach National Wildlife Refuge post volunteers near it from dawn to dusk during nesting season. Whenever crows or other flying predators swoop too close, the volunteers rattle stone-filled cans to scare them away.

The nearly thirteen-thousand-acre Patuxent refuge—where the visitor center conference room is named after Duck Stamp Contest winner and later program administrator Robert Hines, who is credited with turning the contest into an open event by inviting collector William Webster to watch the judging in 1966—is covered mostly by forest and is not known as a waterfowl habitat. Still, federal officials built ponds, then built little islands in the middle of the ponds, just to put some water between foxes and other predators and the few thousand ducks a day that stop by during migration season.

At the Minnesota Valley National Wildlife Refuge, twenty-four hundred acres of which lie beneath the final approach path of Minneapolis–St. Paul International Airport, Fish and Wildlife officials periodically conduct prescribed burns to clear seedling trees and brush in order to open up "singing ground" where male woodcocks can conduct their elaborate courtship ritual during mating season.

Those small battles for conservation are fought daily against the backdrop of a much larger fight. Agricultural innovations such as genetically modified crops and other new technologies

now allow farmers to convert previously unsuitable native wetlands and grasslands into farmland for corn, soybeans, and other
crops. As a result, throughout the critical Prairie Pothole Region, the duck factory of North America, federal planners are
waging a quiet and mostly unseen war to conserve an additional twelve million acres of habitat that they consider critical
for maintaining a healthy population of breeding waterfowl.[2]
The war is waged from federal realty offices; the weapons
are aerial surveillance, rigorous analysis of bird population
projections, land purchases and easements, and public-private
conservation partnerships.

The results of such intense wildlife management are as undeniable as they are inspirational. The National Wildlife Refuge System is considered the crown jewel among the world's
great environmental success stories. With stunningly clear
foresight—and using money generated by the sale of Federal
Duck Stamps[3]—conservation visionaries during the past century have assembled a series of protected havens that serve as safe
stepping-stones for migrating birds that otherwise might have
no habitat left, or might have been hunted to extinction for
reasons as frivolous as a public demand for feathered hats.

Those refuges are home to more than 700 species of birds,
220 mammal species, 250 reptile and amphibian species, and
more than 200 species of fish. Fifty-nine of the refuges were set
up with the primary purpose of preserving threatened or endangered animals.[4] Without such refuges, the American bald
eagle, the very symbol of the United States, likely would exist
only in photographs and as an engraved image on the nation's
quarter coin, because by 1963 the number of breeding pairs in

the lower forty-eight states had slipped to only 417. By 2007, the eagle population had rebounded dramatically enough that the federal government removed it from the endangered species list. In 2010, Fish and Wildlife estimated that there were ten thousand breeding bald eagle pairs.[5]

If you're one of those people who consider conserving species and maintaining a healthy ecosystem unimportant, irrelevant, or the misguided altruism of softheaded, khaki-rumped nature weenies, you might want to consider the economic impact of the refuge system. As detailed in a Fish and Wildlife report titled "Banking on Nature,"[6] nearly forty-one million people visit national wildlife refuges each year. Each of the fifty states has at least one refuge, and there's one within an hour's drive of most major U.S. cities. In the report, federal officials estimated that spending by refuge visitors in fiscal year 2006 generated nearly $1.7 billion in sales for regional economies as hunters and fishermen spent lavishly on their sports—and yes, those activities are legal and controlled in many refuges—and birders bought the high-priced binoculars, field guides, and other supplies they need to watch the annual congregations of migrating species. Refuge visitors spent their cash at local restaurants and hotels, campgrounds, and rental car agencies, supporting jobs for an estimated twenty-seven thousand people and generating $542 million in employment income.

"We've always known that national wildlife refuges enrich American lives," said present-day Ducks Unlimited CEO Dale Hall, who was the director of the Fish and Wildlife Service at the time of the report. "This report reveals that the refuge system, while admirably fulfilling its conservation mission, also repays us in dollars and cents. Those economic benefits go far beyond the system's mandated mission to ensure wild creatures will always have a place on the American landscape."

By late January 2011, just three months after the contest finals in Berkeley, the familiar annual cycles that underpin the Federal Duck Stamp Contest have begun again. Various migrations also are under way, not all of them involving birds.

True, at the Seal Beach National Wildlife Refuge, a massive squadron of Canada geese is honking its way toward a midwinter landing not far from the visitor center where refuge manager Kirk Gilligan is putting away his hatboxes until the next monthly tour. A flock of wigeon dabbles in a nearby marsh pond, and a great blue heron surveys the scene from high atop a tree.

But people are on the move as well. Dan Ashe, the former deputy director of the U.S. Fish and Wildlife Service, who announced the Duck Stamp Contest winners from the Brower Center auditorium podium, is settling into his new role as the federal agency's top official, succeeding Dale Hall, who left to become CEO of Ducks Unlimited, the Federal Duck Stamp Program's most significant private partner. President Obama nominated Ashe for the post just weeks after the 2010 contest,[7] and his move into that leadership role seemed to cap a steady, career-long climb up a bureaucratic ladder.

Paul Schmidt, the assistant director of the service's Migratory Bird Program, has followed Hall out of the public sector coop, landing as Ducks Unlimited's chief conservation officer. In that role, he plans to lead the group's national and international conservation programs and serve as a member of the senior executive team, as well as oversee all public policy and science. Jerome Ford, one of Schmidt's deputies, was promoted into his boss's old job. Pilot and biologist Thom Lewis, who advised the 2010 contest judges, was, like his predecessor in that role, killed in a plane crash, just three months before the 2011 contest was scheduled to begin.

And by the time the injured Brett Favre finally retires in January 2011, after twenty NFL seasons, his public image has taken a serious hit. The NFL has fined him fifty thousand dollars for not cooperating in an investigation into allegations that he sent lewd messages and anatomically detailed photos to a female employee of the New York Jets whom he was trying to woo.[8] Undaunted, Pat Fisher continues her search for a high-profile duck stamp spokesperson. But Favre? "I think we're going to wait and see how everything evolves with his life and reputation before approaching him."

For the fourth time, winner Jim Hautman has launched into his yearlong stint as the Federal Duck Stamp Artist, with scheduled appearances at various wildlife art and conservation events around the country. While he has to sit out the next three contests, Bob and Joe Hautman already have joined hundreds of other competitors in weighing early—and critical—decisions about which bird to paint for 2011. Bob wastes no time in his search for a competitive edge, speculating about which of the year's five eligible species—mallard, wood duck, blue-winged teal, cinnamon teal, and gadwall—might be the best choice.

"Sixty percent of the entries will be mallards," he says, and you can almost hear him calculating the benefits of zagging while most others zig.

The 2011 contest is to be held at the National Conservation Training Center in Shepherdstown, West Virginia, its first occurrence in that state. Might the judging panel once again be drawn from the region where the finals will be held? Which of the five eligible birds might most appeal to such a panel?

Southern California artist Mark Berger arrived at an important crossroads in his life shortly after the 2010 contest ended. Until then, he'd pursued painting as a sideline, dreaming of the day when he could wind down his aerospace career and paint full-time. As soon as he was eligible to retire from his job at Boeing, the fifty-six-year-old rocket scientist filed the necessary paperwork to begin his transition into a new career as full-time artist and part-time aerospace consultant. Among the twenty-five or so guests who toasted his leap during a retirement party Berger hosted at his home in early January 2011 were fellow Federal Duck Stamp Contest veterans Robert Richert and Robert Copple, who'd first told Berger about the contest and sparked his competitive fire. Berger had another reason to celebrate as well. Despite his discouraging assessment of his painting's performance during the second round of judging, his flying geese had received enough points for him to be included, for the second year in a row, among the twenty-five top point-getters eligible for the national tour.

Scot Storm, the equally competitive former college wrestler and architect who won the federal contest in 2003, says he started considering designs for next year's contest as soon as the 2010 judging was over. Not that he didn't dwell on the moment: "I always get a bit agitated when I don't win, no matter how big or small a contest it is. I'm competitive. It's part of the driving force."

He insists his agitation has nothing to do with his competitors; Storm is competing mostly against himself. And he tries to stay philosophical. "In this line of work, nothing is a guarantee. It's five humans judging artwork that tells the story. You just have to be on top of your game." He'll approach the 2011 contest as he's approached all the others: "Analyze it the best you can in the design phase, and let the paint fly."[9]

And back in Arlington, Virginia, the three women who run the Federal Duck Stamp Program are, as always, hard at work. They're not just attending to the details of the upcoming Junior Duck Stamp Contest, scheduled for the following April at the John Heinz National Wildlife Refuge, in Philadelphia, but also planning for the first-day-of-sale ceremony for the stamp made from Jim Hautman's specklebelly painting. It's scheduled for June at a Bass Pro outlet in Katy, Texas.

Hovering above all the activity, though, are those nagging questions about the program's future. Fewer hunters and stamp collectors means fewer stamps sold, and therefore less money available to conserve wetland habitat and build the refuge system. Even with a proposed boost in the sale price of the now fifteen-dollar stamp, there's an unmistakable sense that the ground beneath the grand idea is eroding. Since record-high sales of nearly two and a half million duck stamps in 1971–1972, the number of stamps sold has been in almost steady decline. About a million fewer stamps were sold in 2010 than during the program's heyday. And the U.S. Congress continues to move inexorably toward passing legislation that would expand an eight-state pilot program making electronic duck stamps available nationwide.

Which is one reason why Pat Fisher, the Federal Duck Stamp Program's most passionate advocate, remains worried that the program is slipping into the shadows of American culture.

With her retirement date set for November 2011, she's still waiting for the perfect celebrity spokesman to step forward to help create awareness-raising public-service ads, someone who understands the duck stamp and is eager to take it on as their cause. But by the time Fisher steps down, her fantasy seems as unlikely as a Favre comeback. News of the death of grande dame duck stamp collector Jeanette Cantrell Rudy just two days before the August 2011 deadline adds to the foreboding mood, as does the departure of Junior Duck Stamp Coordinator Elizabeth Jackson for a job at the National Park Service, leaving the program's marketing director, Laurie Shaffer, alone in the Federal Duck Stamp Office, hoping those vacant positions eventually will be filled. The indefatigable Duck Stamp Program has survived countless down cycles during its nearly eight decades, but even the September unveiling of Ducks Unlimited's "Double Up for the Ducks" initiative—which urges duck hunters and other waterfowl enthusiasts to buy two duck stamps instead of just one—feels like a cry for help.

It's not surprising, then, that some of the faithful look back fondly to 2008, when public awareness of the Federal Duck Stamp Program may have—accidentally—reached its zenith.

That year, the card that held the self-adhesive version of the duck stamp made from Joe Hautman's northern pintails was printed with an incorrect phone number for ordering more stamps. Instead of connecting callers to 1-800-STAMP24, the card, owing to the erroneous transposition of two numbers, connected callers to 1-800-TRAMP24, where, according to one published account, "a breathy woman [promised] callers that they could 'talk only to the girls who turn you on' for $1.99 per minute."[10] The faux pas even had one late-night talk show host quipping about duck stamps to a massive audience on national TV.

Reprinting the cards would have cost the agency about three hundred thousand dollars, according to Fish and Wildlife spokeswoman Rachel Levin, and absolutely no one thought it was worth diverting that money from habitat conservation to correct the unfortunate mistake.

But it's hard to think of a time when the groundbreaking, critical, and increasingly obscure Federal Duck Stamp Program had ever got so much attention. And, truth be told, some of the people looking back on that strange, high-profile moment in duck stamp history sound almost wistful about it now.

# APPENDIX A

## How to Buy a Duck Stamp

Preserving the Federal Duck Stamp Program and ensuring the future of wetlands habitat conservation in America is as simple and elegant as the program itself: Just buy a duck stamp every year. They're available through your local post office and at most major sporting goods stores that sell hunting and fishing licenses. You also can order yours online at www.duckstamp.com.

# APPENDIX B

## The Federal Duck Stamp Artists

Listed by year in which the stamp made from
their painting was released.

Jay N. "Ding" Darling (1934)

Frank W. Benson (1935)

Richard E. Bishop (1936)

Joseph D. Knap (1937)

Roland H. Clark (1938)

Lynn B. Hunt (1939)

Francis L. Jaques (1940)

Edwin R. Kalmbach (1941)

A. Lassell Ripley (1942)

Walter E. Bohl (1943)

Walter A. Weber (1944)

Owen J. Gromme (1945)

Robert W. Hines (1946)

Jack Murray (1947)

Maynard Reece (1948)

Roger E. Preuss (1949)

Walter A. Weber (1950)

Maynard Reece (1951)

John H. Dick (1952)

Clayton B. Seagears (1953)

Harvey D. Sandstrom (1954)

Stanley Stearns (1955)

Edward J. Bierly (1956)

Jackson M. Abbott (1957)

Leslie C. Kouba (1958)

Maynard Reece (1959)

John A. Ruthven (1960)

Edward A. Morris (1961)

Edward A. Morris (1962)

Edward J. Bierly (1963)

Stanley Stearns (1964)

Ron Jenkins (1965)

Stanley Stearns (1966)

Leslie C. Kouba (1967)

Claremont G. Pritchard (1968)

Maynard Reece (1969)

Edward J. Bierly (1970)

Maynard Reece (1971)

Arthur M. Cook (1972)

Lee LeBlanc (1973)

David A. Maass (1974)

James P. Fisher (1975)

Alderson Magee (1976)

Martin R. Murk (1977)

Albert Gilbert (1978)

Ken Michaelsen (1979)

Richard Plasschaert (1980)

John S. Wilson (1981)

David A. Maass (1982)

Phil Scholer (1983)

William C. Morris (1984)

Gerald Mobley (1985)

Burton E. Moore (1986)

Arthur G. Anderson (1987)

Daniel Smith (1988)

Neal R. Anderson (1989)

James Hautman (1990)

Nancy Howe (1991)

Joseph Hautman (1992)

Bruce Miller (1993)

Neal R. Anderson (1994)

James Hautman (1995)

Wilhelm Goebel (1996)

Robert Hautman (1997)

Robert Steiner (1998)

James Hautman (1999)

Adam Grimm (2000)

Robert Hautman (2001)

Joseph Hautman (2002)

Ron Louque (2003)

Scot Storm (2004)

Mark Anderson (2005)

Sherrie Russell Meline (2006)

Richard C. Clifton (2007)

Joseph Hautman (2008)

Joshua Spies (2009)

Robert Bealle (2010)

James Hautman (2011)

Joseph Hautman (2012)

# APPENDIX C

## The Imitators

According to the National Duck Stamp Collectors Society, thirty-four U.S. states were issuing wildlife conservation stamps modeled after the Federal Duck Stamp during the 2010 contest year.

Alabama
Alaska
Arizona
Arkansas
California
Colorado
Connecticut
Delaware
Illinois
Indiana
Iowa
Louisiana
Maine
Maryland

Massachusetts
Michigan
Minnesota
Missouri
Nevada
North Carolina
North Dakota
Ohio
Oklahoma
Oregon
Pennsylvania
Rhode Island
South Carolina
Tennessee
Texas
Vermont
Virginia
Washington
Wisconsin
Wyoming

# ACKNOWLEDGMENTS

Writing a book about pro-am competitive duck painting may seem like an odd undertaking for someone who knows very little about art and even less about ducks. I was able to do so only with the help of many people, none of whom ever smirked at my ignorance as I pestered them with questions.

My friend Mark Berger first introduced me to the wonders of the Federal Duck Stamp Contest during a Saturday-morning bike ride in October 2009, and his enthusiasm as an artist and contest competitor was such that I, too, was lured down the rabbit hole. I owe him a great debt.

Many other artists took the time to share their insights and stories, including Robert Bealle; Robert Copple; Adam Grimm; Karen, Rebecca, and Bonnie Latham; Rob McBroom; Sherrie Russell Meline; Bruce Miller; Gerald Mobley; Robert Richert; Scot Storm; and, of course, the Hautman brothers, Joe, Bob, and Jim, who are every bit as talented and nice as one might hope dynastic duck stamp champions would be.

Patricia Fisher, Elizabeth Jackson, and Laurie Shaffer—the self-described "three blondes" of the Federal Duck Stamp

Program in 2010—were exactly the kind of government employees that Americans deserve: dedicated, conscientious, thrifty, and committed to the highest ideals of public service. We were lucky to have them, as well as Fish and Wildlife spokeswoman Rachel Levin, who was an invaluable help with fact-checking. Ducks Unlimited CEO and former Fish and Wildlife director Dale Hall was equally generous with his time, and is no less dedicated in his role at the helm of the program's private-sector partner in conserving America's wetlands. I'm also grateful to Fish and Wildlife director Dan Ashe for so effectively articulating his passion for the program, and to visitor services librarian Judy Geck of the Minnesota Valley National Wildlife Refuge; Brad Knudsen, manager of the Patuxent Research Refuge, in Laurel, Maryland; and Kirk Gilligan at the Seal Beach National Wildlife Refuge for showing me around those special places.

Retired Fish and Wildlife pilot and biologist John Solberg was heroically patient while schooling me in the ways of waterfowl, specifically the five eligible species featured in the 2010 contest. David Allen Sibley, author of what may be the planet's finest field guides to birds, offered valuable insights into and perspective on the world of bird art, and *WildBird* editor Amy K. Hooper helped me understand the critical role the birding community must play in the future of the Duck Stamp Program.

I benefited enormously from the wisdom of those who've helped create and maintain the public passion for duck stamps, including Rita and Bob Dumaine of the Sam Houston Duck Company and the National Duck Stamp Collectors Society, and collectors William Webster, founder of Wild Wings, and Jeanette Cantrell Rudy, whose comments about duck stamps and her collection of them are available for public viewing in a series of remarkable videos archived on the website of the Smithsonian's National Postal Museum.

My friend and longtime writing partner, Patrick J. Kiger, helped me report the magazine article that led to this book by acting as my eyes and ears during the judging of the 2009 Duck Stamp Contest, at the Patuxent Research Refuge.

My editorial colleagues at *Orange Coast* magazine—including Mindy Benham, Chris Christensen, Carly Hebert, Justin Patrick Long, Anne Valdespino, and Jim Walters—also helped me create the article that preceded this book, and it's my privilege to be part of that team. In addition, Deborah Paul and Greg Loewen of Emmis Communications were unfailingly gracious and supportive.

Susan Ginsburg at Writers House, my longtime literary agent, was the first to believe in the potential of this story, and I might never have proposed the idea without her early encouragement. We both believed there'd be a smart editor out there who would understand its rich potential, and we were right. Jacqueline Johnson at Walker & Company has been a terrific partner in giving the book its final form. I'm grateful to them both. Feedback from the members of my writing group, the Mavericks, was invaluable as the manuscript took shape, and copy editor Lynn Rapoport was a godsend.

On a more personal note, my wife, Judy, to whom this book is dedicated, made it all possible by putting up with more than a year of my six-day workweeks as I traveled, reported, and wrote this book around the demands of my day job. After thirty years, she remains, to me, endlessly fascinating. Also, this, my sixth book, is the first one I've written without the competing obligations and time commitments of having children in the house. To our fledglings, Lanie and Parker, I want you both to know something that I learned during the yearlong effort to deliver this story about the wonderful and often peculiar world of competitive duck painting: Empty nests are vastly overrated.

Martin J. Smith
Palos Verdes Estates, California

# NOTES

## PROLOGUE

1. U.S. Department of the Interior, *Budget Justifications and Performance Information Fiscal Year 2012*, accessed January 28, 2012, http://www.fws.gov/budget/2012/FWS%202012%20Budget %20Justifications.pdf.
2. U.S. Fish and Wildlife Service, Federal Duck Stamp Office, "How Do Duck Stamps Benefit Wildlife?," accessed January 11, 2011, http://www.fws.gov/duckstamps/Info/Stamps/ stampinfo.htm.

## *Chapter 1:* THE HUNTERS GATHER

1. Carolyn Jones, "Stamp Contest Could Running Afoul in Berkeley," SFGate.com, June 8, 2010, http://articles.sfgate .com/2010-06-08/bay-area/21781408_1_federal-duck -stamp-contest-duck-hunters-federal-wildlife-refuges.
2. Richard C. Paddock, "Curtain Falls on Tree Protest," *Los Angeles Times*, September 10, 2008, http://articles.latimes .com/2008/sep/10/local/me-trees10.

3. Scott Weidensaul, *Duck Stamps: Art in the Service of Conservation* (New York: Gallery Books, 1989), 17.

4. Eric Jay Dolin and Bob Dumaine, *The Duck Stamp Story* (Iola, WI: Krause Publications, 2000), 70.

5. Patrick Condon, "Wildlife Artists Seek Success in Stamp Contests," Associated Press, July 27, 2009.

6. U.S. Fish and Wildlife Service, National Wildlife Refuge System, "Welcome to the National Wildlife Refuge System," accessed May 16, 2011, http://www.fws.gov/refuges.

7. U.S. Department of the Interior, *Budget Justifications and Performance Information Fiscal Year 2012,* accessed January 28, 2012, http://www.fws.gov/budget/2012/FWS%202012%20Budget %20Justifications.pdf.

8. Dolin and Dumaine, *The Duck Stamp Story*, 20.

9. Russell A. Fink and Jean Pride Stearns, *Duck Stamp Prints* (Lorton, VA: privately published by Russell A. Fink, 1985), 116.

*Chapter 2:* THE FIRST BATTLE
OF SPECKLEBELLY

1. U.S. Fish and Wildlife Service, Federal Duck Stamp Office, "2010 Federal Duck Stamp Contest Information, Entry Form and Regulations," accessed January 28, 2012, http://www.fws .gov/duckstamps/federal/pdf/DuckStampRegs2010.pdf, 3.

2. "Brant," Cornell Lab of Ornithology, accessed January 28, 2012, http://www.allaboutbirds.org/guide/brant/id.

3. "Northern Shoveler," Ducks Unlimited, accessed January 28, 2012, http://www.ducks.org/hunting/waterfowl-id/northern -shoveler.

4. Ibid.

5. "Ruddy Duck," Ducks Unlimited, accessed January 28, 2012, http://www.ducks.org/hunting/waterfowl-id/ruddy-duck.

6. Tina Susman, "Geese Pay Price for Their Success," *Los Angeles Times*, August 2, 2010.

7. "Canada Goose," Ducks Unlimited, accessed January 28, 2012, http://www.ducks.org/hunting/waterfowl-id/canada-goose.

8. "White-fronted Goose," Ducks Unlimited, accessed January 28, 2012, http://www.ducks.org/hunting/waterfowl-id/white-fronted-goose.

### Chapter 3: GUNS, GREED, AND THE GRAND IDEA

1. Eric Jay Dolin and Bob Dumaine, *The Duck Stamp Story* (Iola, WI: Krause Publications, 2000), 12.

2. Ibid.

3. Ibid., 13.

4. "Chart of US population, 1790–2000," Census-Charts.com, accessed June 18, 2011, http://www.census-charts.com/Population/pop-us-1790-2000.html.

5. Dolin and Dumaine, *The Duck Stamp Story*, 17.

6. Ibid.

7. *American Buffalo: Spirit of a Nation: Introduction, Nature*, PBS, accessed June 18, 2011, http://www.pbs.org/wnet/nature/episodes/american-buffalo-spirit-of-a-nation/introduction/2183.

8. Ibid.

9. Dolin and Dumaine, *The Duck Stamp Story*, 20.

10. Tim Rutten, "Why Print Survives," *Los Angeles Times*, December 11, 2010.

11. "World's Most Expensive Book Goes Up for Sale," BBC News, September 9, 2010, http://www.bbc.co.uk/news/entertainment-arts-11242275.

12. *Martin v. Waddell*, 41 U.S. 367 (1842), accessed January 28, 2012, http://supreme.justia.com/us/41/367/case.html.

13. "History of Audubon and Waterbird Conservation," *Audubon*, accessed June 18, 2011, http://birds.audubon.org/history-audubon-and-waterbird-conservation.

14. "Audubon Turns 100," *Audubon*, accessed June 18, 2011, http://www.audubon.org/centennial.

15. Dolin and Dumaine, *The Duck Stamp Story*, 25.

16. Article 1, section 8, clause 3 of the U.S. Constitution reads, "To regulate Commerce with foreign Nations, and among the several States, and with the Indian Tribes." http://www.house.gov/house/Constitution/Constitution.html.

17. U.S. Fish and Wildlife Service, Migratory Bird Program, "A Guide to the Laws and Treaties of the United States for Protecting Migratory Birds," accessed January 28, 2012, http://www.fws.gov/migratorybirds/RegulationsPolicies/treatlaw.html.

18. "Jay Norwood 'Ding' Darling (1876–1962)," accessed June 18, 2011, http://www.dingdarling.org/about.html.

19. Richard A. Posner, ed., *The Essential Holmes: Selections from the Letters, Speeches, Judicial Opinions, and Other Writings of Oliver Wendell Holmes, Jr.* (Chicago: University of Chicago Press, 1992), 295.

20. Dolin and Dumaine, *The Duck Stamp Story*, 31.

21. "Black Sunday: April 14, 1935," *American Experience*, PBS, accessed June 18, 2011, http://www.pbs.org/wgbh/ameri canexperience/features/general-article/dustbowl-black -sunday.

22. Dolin and Dumaine, *The Duck Stamp Story*, 34.

23. Ibid., 40.

24. Ibid.

25. Ibid., 43.

26. U.S. Department of the Interior, *Budget Justifications and Performance Information Fiscal Year 2012*, accessed January 28, 2012, http://www.fws.gov/budget/2012/FWS%202012%20Bud get%20Justifications.pdf.

## *Chapter 4:* ROUND ONE

1. U.S. Fish and Wildlife Service, "Small Wetlands Program: A Half Century of Conserving Prairie Habitat," May 6, 2008.

2. Ibid.

3. U.S. Government Accountability Office, *Prairie Pothole Region: Report to the Subcommittee on Interior, Environment, and Related Agencies, Committee on Appropriations, House of Representatives*, September 2007, accessed January 20, 2012.

## *Chapter 5:* THE SECOND BATTLE OF SPECKLEBELLY

1. U.S. Fish and Wildlife Service, Federal Duck Stamp Office, *Statistical Report on Duck Stamp Contest Entries*, 2010 Federal Duck Stamp Contest brochure, October 15–16, 2010.

2. "Sutter Buttes, California, USA," About.com, accessed June 18, 2011, http://geology.about.com/library/bl/peaks/blsutterbuttes.htm.

3. "Championship Clubs," MLB.com, accessed June 18, 2011, http://mlb.mlb.com/nyy/history/championships.jsp.

4. Department of the Interior, "Federal Wildlife Agency Announces 1972 Duck Stamp Contest," August 29, 1971.

5. Russell A. Fink and Jean Pride Stearns, *Duck Stamp Prints* (Lorton, VA: privately published by Russell A. Fink, 1985), 116.

Chapter 7: THE POWER OF THE PRIZE

1. Eric Jay Dolin and Bob Dumaine, *The Duck Stamp Story* (Iola, WI: Krause Publications, 2000), 142.

2. Ibid.

3. Russell A. Fink and Jean Pride Stearns, *Duck Stamp Prints* (Lorton, VA: privately published by Russell A. Fink, 1985), 26.

4. Dolin and Dumaine, *The Duck Stamp Story*, 141.

Chapter 8: ROUND TWO

1. U.S. Fish and Wildlife Service, Federal Duck Stamp Office, "2011 Federal Duck Stamp Contest Information, Entry Form and Regulations," accessed June 18, 2011, http://www.fws.gov/duckstamps/federal/pdf/DuckStampRegs11.pdf.

2. Kelly Burgess, "Waterfowl Survey Plane Crash Kills Two U.S. Fish and Wildlife Service Biologists," *Los Angeles Times*, Outposts blog, January 20, 2010, http://latimesblogs.latimes

.com/outposts/2010/01/us-fish-and-wildlife-service-biolo
gists-killed-in-plane-crash.html.

Chapter 9: WHAT IS ART, ANYWAY?

1. Jean Clottes, "Ancient Grand Masters," *Time Europe*, July 4–
   11, 2005.
2. Ronald Baenninger, "Vanishing Species: The Disappearance of Animals from Western Art," *Anthrozoös: A Multidis-
   ciplinary Journal of the Interactions of People & Animals* 1, no. 2
   (1987): 85–89.
3. Ted Williams, "Miss America Contest of Wildlife Art,"
   *Audubon*, July 1990, 22–29.
4. Donegan Optical Company Inc., accessed January 28, 2012,
   http://www.doneganoptical.com/optivisor.php.
5. "U.S. Postal Service Is in 'Serious Jeopardy,'" *Los Angeles
   Times*, November 13, 2010.
6. "Glorious Flight: The Jeanette C. Rudy Duck Stamp Collection: I Collect Duck Stamps!," Smithsonian National
   Postal Museum, http://www.postalmuseum.si.edu/Jeanette
   RudyInterview/video1.html.
7. Eric Jay Dolin and Bob Dumaine, *The Duck Stamp Story*
   (Iola, WI: Krause Publications, 2000), 142.
8. "Glorious Flight: The Jeanette C. Rudy Duck Stamp Collection: Jeanette C. Rudy's Legacy," Smithsonian National
   Postal Museum, accessed January 28, 2012, http://www
   .postalmuseum.si.edu/JeanetteRudyInterview/video6.html.
9. Scott Weidensaul, *Duck Stamps: Art in the Service of Conservation* (New York: Gallery Books, 1989), 17.

10. Tim Taylor, "2010 Federal Duck Stamp Entries," Wet Canvas, September 21, 2010, www.wetcanvas.com/forums/showthread.php?t=703521.


### Chapter 10: ROUND THREE

1. "Brant," Ducks Unlimited, accessed January 28, 2012, http://www.ducks.org/hunting/waterfowl-id/brant.
2. The Works of Kip Richmond, accessed June 18, 2011, http://www.kiprichmond.org/index.html.


### Chapter 11: THE LOOMING THREATS

1. Richard Louv, *Last Child in the Woods* (Chapel Hill, N.C.: Algonquin Books of Chapel Hill, 2005), front matter.
2. Richard Louv, "Children and Nature Movement: How a Movement Is Forming and How You Can Get Involved," accessed June 18, 2011, http://richardlouv.com/last-child -movement.
3. Louv, *Last Child*, 117.
4. "Number of U.S. Hunters Dwindles," *USA Today*, September 2, 2007, http://www.usatoday.com/news/nation/envi ronment/2007-09-02-fewer-hunters_N.htm.
5. Richard Louv, *Last Child in the Woods*, updated and expanded edition (New York: Workman Books, 2008).
6. "Ducks Unlimited and Hunting," Ducks Unlimited, accessed January 28, 2012, http://ducks.org/hunting.
7. "Fish and Game Q&A: New Computer Licenses Draw Queries," *Los Angeles Times*, Outposts blog, January 6, 2011,

http://latimesblogs.latimes.com/outposts/2011/01/fish-and
-game-q-a.html.


*Chapter 12:* THE HUNTER-HUGGER SCHISM

1. "Causes of Bird Mortality," Sibley Guides, accessed January 15, 2010, http://www.sibleyguides.com/conservation/causes-of-bird-mortality.
2. Mike Bergin, "Time to Buy a Duck Stamp . . . or Not," 10,000 Birds, July 1, 2009, http://10000birds.com/time-to-buy-a-duck-stamp-or-not.htm.
3. U.S. Fish and Wildlife Service, National Wildlife Refuge System, "Do Hunters Pay for the Lands Acquired for the National Wildlife Refuge System?," accessed June 18, 2011, http://www.fws.gov/refuges/about/acquisition.html.
4. Jeffrey A. Gordon, "Are Birders Really Buying 92% of the Duck Stamps Sold?," August 25, 2010, http://jeffreyago rdon.com/2010/08/are-birders-really-buying-92-of-duck-stamps-sold.


*Chapter 13:* JUDGMENT DAY:
THE TIEBREAK ROUND

1. "Disco Duck by Rick Dees and His Cast of Idiots," Songfacts.com, accessed January 28, 2012, http://www.songfacts.com/detail.php?id=6796.
2. Russell A. Fink and Jean Pride Stearns, *Duck Stamp Prints* (Lorton, VA: privately published by Russell A. Fink, 1985).

Chapter 14: WHERE THE WILD THINGS ARE

1. Smithsonian National Zoological Park, "Roseate Spoonbill Fact Sheet," accessed January 28, 2012, http://nationalzoo.si .edu/Animals/Birds/Facts/FactSheets/fact-rosespoonbill .cfm.

2. U.S. Government Accountability Office, *Prairie Pothole Region: Report to the Subcommittee on Interior, Environment, and Related Agencies, Committee on Appropriations, House of Representatives*, September 2007, 22.

3. Ibid., 14.

4. U.S. Fish and Wildlife Service, National Wildlife Refuge System, "Welcome to the National Wildlife Refuge System," accessed February 23, 2010, http://www.fws.gov/ refuges/about/welcome.html.

5. "Eagle Sightings Skyrocket," *Los Angeles Times*, December 16, 2010.

6. U.S. Fish and Wildlife Service, National Wildlife Refuge System, "Banking on Nature 2006: Economic Benefits to Local Communities of National Wildlife Refuge Visitation," accessed January 28, 2012, http://www.fws.gov/refuges/ about/bankingonnature.html.

7. U.S. Department of the Interior, "Secretary Salazar Applauds President's Nomination of Dan Ashe to Be Director of the U.S. Fish and Wildlife Service," December 3, 2010, http://www.fws.gov/midwest/News/release.cfm?rid=313.

8. Frank Pingue, "Factbox: Favre Officially Files for Third Retirement," Reuters, January 17, 2011, http://www.reuters .com/article/idUSTRE70G56W20110117?pageNumber=2.

9. Scot Storm, via e-mail, April 29, 2011.

10. Paul Walsh, "Duck Stamp Includes Phone-Sex Number," *Minneapolis—St. Paul Star Tribune*, September 5, 2008, www .startribune.com/local/27822694.html?elr=KArksLckD8E QDUoaEyqyP4O:DW3ckUiD3aPc:_Yyc:aULPQL7 PQLanchO7DiUss.

# LIST OF ILLUSTRATIONS

# INDEX

# A NOTE ON THE AUTHOR

MARTIN J. SMITH is a veteran writer and magazine editor who has received more than fifty awards for his journalistic work and been nominated for three prestigious fiction awards for his crime novels. Also the coauthor of two previous nonfiction books about pop culture history, Smith decided to write about the Federal Duck Stamp Program because in it he sees a ray of hope and living reminder of what the American federal government once was, and someday could be again: visionary, idealistic, and inarguably effective. He lives in Southern California. Visit this book's website at www.wildduckchase.com.